TIME IS MONEY!

Drawing by Robert Byrd; reprinted by permission of Western Savings Bank, Philadelphia.

TIME IS MONEY!

The Key to Managerial Success

Ross A. Webber

 THE FREE PRESS
A Division of Macmillan Publishing Co., Inc.
NEW YORK

Collier Macmillan Publishers
LONDON

THE FREE PRESS
A Division of Macmillan Publishing Co., Inc.
866 Third Avenue, New York, N.Y.   10022

Collier Macmillan Canada, Ltd.

Library of Congress Catalog Card Number: 80-1032

Printed in the United States of America

printing number

1   2   3   4   5   6   7   8   9   10

Library of Congress Cataloging in Publication Data

Webber, Ross A
  Time is money!

  Includes index.
  1. Time allocation. 2. Management. I. Title.
HD38.W396   658.4′093   80-1032
ISBN 0-02-934030-6

Various proprietors of copyright have granted permission to reprint previously published material. Thanks are due to all those named in credit lines for the cartoons that appear throughout the book and to those named in the following acknowledgments of sources.

The poem on page 7 is from Michel Quoist, *Prayers,* translated from *Prières* by Michel Quoist (New York: Sheed & Ward, 1963), p. 97. Copyright © 1963. Reprinted by permission of Andrews & McMeel, Inc., Mission, Kansas, and of Les Editions Ouvrières, Paris.

The credo on pages 76–77 is reprinted by permission of Johnson & Johnson. Copyright Johnson & Johnson 1979.

Figure 1 is from Joseph Trickett, "A More Effective Use of Time," *California Management Review,* vol. 4, no. 4 (Summer 1962), p. 7. Copyright © 1962 by the Regents of the University of California. Reprinted only by permission of the Regents.

Figure 3 is from R. Alec Mackenzie, *The Time Trap: Managing Your Way Out* (New York: Amacom, 1972), p. 23. Copyright © 1972 by Amacom, a division of American Management Associations. All rights reserved. Reprinted by permission of the publisher. This figure originally appeared in R. Alec Mackenzie, *Managing Time at the Top* (New York: The President's Association, 1970).

Figures 4, 8–14, and 17 are from Ross A. Webber, *Management: Basic Elements of Managing Organizations,* rev. ed. (Homewood, Ill.: Richard D. Irwin, 1979), pp. 274, 374–77, and 549. Copyright © 1979 by Richard D. Irwin, Inc. Reprinted by permission. Portions of chapters 7, 9, and 10 have been adapted from this book.

Table 2 is from Ross A. Webber, *Time and Management* (New York: Van Nostrand Reinhold, 1972). Copyright © 1972 by Litton Educational Publishing, Inc. Reprinted by permission of Van Nostrand Reinhold Company.

Table 5 has been adapted from Eugene E. Jennings, *The Mobile Manager* (Ann Arbor: Graduate School of Business Administration, University of Michigan, 1967) (New York: McGraw-Hill, 1971).

To Mary Lou

Past, Present, and Future . . .

CONTENTS

PREFACE

"Time is money" was Benjamin Franklin's phrase for dramatizing time's importance by linking it with the most common measure of value. Most of us must exchange our time for wages necessary for survival. And business managers, of course, are especially concerned with using time to generate income and profits. Nonetheless, time is much more important than money. Time is life itself. Ultimately, we want to manage our time more effectively not to make more money but to pursue our highest human aspirations.

This book endeavors to help you on both the mundane and the exalted dimensions of using time. It is divided into two parts, which examine shorter-term and longer-term time. Part One surveys various approaches for managing work time in the short run. Lists, diaries, logs, and time plans are described. Tactics are presented for escaping from drowning in emergencies, expanding discretionary time, and fighting procrastination. The objective of this part is to assist you in becoming a more efficient manager.

Effectiveness is more important than efficiency, however. Accomplishing your objectives should be your aim, not merely keeping busy. The really big time wasters derive less from poor personal time use than from unclear power, ineffective delegation, and passivity toward one's career. Therefore, Part Two presents strategies for self-management in the long run. Delegating more clearly, attacking role stress, defining personal goals, and challenging oneself are all discussed.

The book's content was developed over five years of conducting executive seminars at the Wharton School, University of Pennsylvania. More than a thousand managers and professionals have participated in my two-day sessions on executive self-management. I am indebted to many of these men and women for helpful suggestions. My thanks also to William Zucker, director of Wharton Executive Education, and William Kulok, president of the New York Management Center, Inc., who administer the programs.

The book reflects the helpful editorial contributions of Robert Wallace, Claude Conyers, and Elly Dickason. My thanks also to my daughters Sarah, Judith, and Jennifer, who typed, proofed, and indexed. Cartoons are used extensively to illustrate points and to lend needed humor to the serious topic of managing time. King Features Syndicate, Cartoon Features Syndicate, Universal Press Syndicate, Chicago Tribune–N.Y. News Syndicate, the Sperry Corporation, the Western Savings Bank of Philadelphia, the *New Yorker,* and *Playboy* were especially helpful. To a remarkable extent, working on this book validated the old cliché that "time flies when you're having fun!"

CHAPTER 1

What Does Time Mean to You?

Time is not the same for everyone. As with the inkblot of psychological fame, people project themselves onto their conceptions of time. Time seems to have special meaning for those attracted to managerial careers. To explore the interrelation between personality, culture, and time, let us consider the following tests of time perspectives.

Time and Achievement

No ideal personality guarantees success as a manager. Managers come in all sizes and shapes and with a variety of traits.[1] Nonetheless, people with a substantial need for achievement appear to be attracted to management and to be successful at it.

Attitude tests. Simple tests have been used to determine the high achiever's attitudes toward time.[2] Your responses to the following five typical tests will provide insight into your own attitudes toward time and achievement.

TEST ONE: *Time Metaphors.* Which of the following images most closely fits time in your life?
A quiet, motionless ocean   ___
A galloping horseman   ___

TEST TWO: *Time Description.* Which two of the following words best describe the idea of time for you?

sharp	sad
active	clear
empty	young
soothing	cold
tense	deep

TEST THREE: *Past Events.* How many years have passed since each of the following events?
Outbreak of the Korean war   ___
Cuban missile crisis   ___
Supreme Court decision outlawing
   school segregation   ___
Assassination of Martin Luther King   ___
Resignation of President Nixon   ___

TEST FOUR: *Checking Your Watch*. This simple experiment may suggest how your time perspective is translated into behavior. Check your wristwatch for accuracy. Use the radio or telephone to determine the exact time. Compare the results.

Your watch time   ___

Actual time   ___

    Your watch is   ___ minutes fast/slow.

TEST FIVE: *Perceiving Time*. You will need a helper for this one. Find a quiet room where you will not be disturbed. You should not have any reading matter available or any work to perform. You may listen to quiet music but not to a radio program that announces the time. Before you closet yourself in the room, have a friend agree to call you after a period of time he determines (from ten to thirty minutes). Now go sit and think or dream. When your friend calls, estimate how much time has passed while you were sitting in the room.

Your estimate   ___ minutes

Actual time   ___ minutes

Achievement orientation. The above tests have been given to many people, particularly to determine the need for achievement. People high in this need tend to share certain perspectives on time and tend to gravitate toward careers like management. They crave the satisfaction of completing difficult tasks through persistent effort, of reaching a distant goal by moderately risky action.

Emphasis is less on rewards or honors than on delight in the process itself.[3] Great achievements may bring social prestige, power, security, perhaps even love. As satisfying as such things may be, they do not reflect the need for achievement. People with high achievement needs may like status and money as much as others, but they are centrally concerned with the process of performing a task well, meeting high standards, overcoming difficult obstacles, and trying novel methods.

Movement, direction, and value characterize such individuals' views on time. On Test One, most people with high achievement needs choose a metaphor like "a galloping horseman," denoting speed and action, rather than one of "a quiet, motionless ocean." Complementing this dynamic perspective is the tendency of high achievers to describe time in terms like "clear, young, sharp, active, tense" rather than "empty, soothing, sad, cold, deep."

Your responses probably agree with those of high achievers. Indeed, most Americans would choose similarly. But the residents of a steamy coastal village in India might respond with the image of that empty, deep, motionless ocean.

It appears that people with high achievement needs are more acutely aware of time's passage. They tend to recall the past events in Test Three as nearer the present and tend to underestimate the time that has passed.[4] The actual dates are as follow:

> Outbreak of the Korean war: 1950
> Cuban missile crisis: 1962
> Supreme Court decision outlawing
> 　　school segregation: 1954
> Assassination of Martin Luther King: 1968
> Resignation of President Nixon: 1974

When sitting alone in a room, as in Test Five, high achievement-oriented people tend to overestimate how much time has passed.[5] Those lower in achievement need tend to underestimate—perhaps because they are less active, less impatient, less concerned about lost time, and more likely to become passively absorbed.

But how could attitudes toward time and achievement affect a person's watch? So might be your question in regard to Test Four. Research suggests that people with higher needs for achievement tend to have watches that are fast![6] Unless one believes in the power of human brain waves to influence mechanical reality, this seems remarkable. Yet it is not. Achievement-oriented people frequently set their watches ahead a little, thus attempting to create time, a little game to delude themselves that they are getting ahead of tyrannical time. To individuals with high achievement need, time seems to move faster. They are, so to speak, always a little ahead of themselves by setting their watches ahead of the actual time.

Images of time. Americans' concern for time is all-pervasive. For us, time is a scarce commodity to be used carefully not an endless resource to be consumed carelessly. To picture the matter schematically, we can see time either as a circle or as a straight line. The circle suggests repetition and continuity for time is measured by natural events: the sun's movement, the moon's phases, the seasons, birth, and death. Measurement is gross; minutes and hours have no meaning. If the present is wasted, it will come around again. Today will return tomorrow, for life and time are endless repetition. With such a philosophy life appears unhurried, even serene.

How different is the linear view! Yesterday is gone forever, today is here but a moment, and tomorrow depends on what we do now. Time is associated less with natural phenomena, more with the artificial movement of a mechanical or electronic timepiece. Time becomes measured and referred to as precise points, not ranges. Life appears cluttered and hectic as people respond to time's demands.

The western world's emphasis on progress and growth is symbolized by the image of time as an arrow moving forward in a straight line from an ancient past to an unknown future.[7] The imagery is particularly appropriate for the person of action having to pick an alternative from an array of possibilities before an approaching deadline. The decision is made, the deadline arrives, passes. Now Omar Khayyam's familiar words take on new meaning:

© 1978 Universal Press Syndicate. Reprinted by permission.

The Moving Finger writes; and, having writ,
Moves on: nor all your Piety nor Wit,
    Shall lure it back to cancel half a Line,
Nor all your Tears wash out a Word of it.

Most Americans have been exhorted by moralists to make the most of time: "A waste of time is the worst of sins," "Idle hands are the devil's workshop," and so on. Similarly, after Lenin took power in Russia in 1917, he began to preach that time was to be preserved and used effectively. Whatever superfluity of time that people had enjoyed (or found monotonous) under tsarist rule should not exist for citizens in the new workers' state. Here is an extract from a leaflet distributed by the Soviet Time League, whose members were obliged to protest against and report every waste of time they encountered:

Measure your time, control it!

Do everything on time! Exactly on the minute!

Save time, make time count, work fast![8]

It may not be very poetic, but it is not unlike the philosophy of many American managers.

Time and the Manager

Managers—like all people of action—are particularly subject to time pressures. The first people in Europe to carry personal timepieces after the clock was invented in the seventeenth century were businessmen.[9] Carrying a clock was more than just a symbol of status; it was a mark of wisdom and virtue. Today we say that using time correctly reflects these worthy attributes. To be prudent and concerned about time is a trait we strive to teach our children. Perhaps Marshall McLuhan was correct when he said "The Eskimo is a servomechanism of his kayak, the cowboy of his horse, the businessman of his clock."[10] For many of us the lines of Michel Quoist are all too true:

Good-bye, Sir, excuse me, I haven't time.
I'll come back, I can't wait, I haven't time.
I must end this letter—I haven't time.
I'd love to help you, but I haven't time.
I can't accept, having no time.
I can't think, I can't read, I'm swamped, I haven't time.
I'd like to pray, but I haven't time.[11]

But if time cannot be slowed and the past cannot be re-
stored, can managers do nothing but make their decisions as
they come? Must they always be passive respondents to the
external forces that converge on them demanding action? Of
course not. Although managers cannot be entirely free, they
can and do *manage* at least some of their time. I hope this
book will be of help in this endeavor.

The book is divided into two parts. The first will analyze
how many of us are tyrannized by the present, so busy fighting current fires that we can't take time to prevent future
ones. Many tactics for managing short-run time will be described and evaluated with the aid of lists, logs, and diaries.

The second part examines longer-term time by showing
how the past often dominates our behavior. Policies, procedures, and practices reflect past history without relevance to
present and future problems. We can sleepwalk through our
organizational lives. Various strategies for retaining flexibility and growth will be explored.

I do not want to sound too mechanistic or overly ration-
alistic. I am not attempting to develop fixed rules on how
managers should spend their time. Much of the available
literature on time management suffers from just such bias.[12]
It pictures a cool and rational executive allocating his time
in advance of events according to some objective criteria related to organizational goals. Everything is managed. But
this is impossible. To foster such an image is misleading and
unfair to harried executives. Managers need to hear realistic
talk not more advice telling them to be something they cannot. They are not able to plan and control everything—even
their own time.

A manager has to play many roles. One of these is the

response agent, subject to the control of others. We shall see that total management of a manager's time is not possible or even desirable. Some time cannot and should not be managed. In short, at times managers must drift.

The aim of this book is to assist present and prospective managers in reconciling the tyranny and the promise of time. No panaceas will be offered, no miracles revealed. Time's illimitable flow precludes such possibilities. Nonetheless, in an area so vital even small advances are large in importance. Perhaps the discussion of the manager's use of time will bring a sense of familiarity or trigger a shock of recognition. Good. Analysis may make explicit many things taken for granted. More important, reading, talking, and thinking about these matters will free us a little from time's restraints.

PART ONE
MANAGING SHORTER-TERM TIME

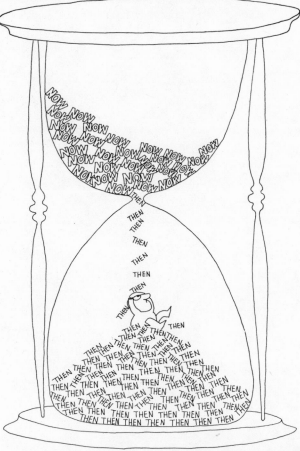

CHAPTER 2

How the Present Tyrannizes

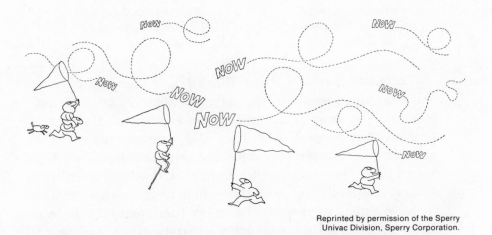

Reprinted by permission of the Sperry
Univac Division, Sperry Corporation.

When your home is burning, you rightly don't stop to figure out how the fire started or how the next one might be prevented. You focus on the present, deciding whether to fight or flee the flames. "The only reality is the present" goes an old Indian proverb. And it is true. Yet, if a manager pays attention only to the present, he will be out of control; life will be expended responding to events that spring like robbers out of a deep wood.

And there are plenty of villains. When asked to describe what wastes their time, managers mention one or more of the following items:

misplaced material	unnecessary outgoing
visitors	correspondence
unanticipated interruptions	incoming telephone calls
commuting	poor organizational
long letters	structure
waiting for people	coffee breaks
failure to delegate	procrastination
mediocre personnel	preparing unnecessary
trivial matters	reports that go unread
high-level meetings on	talks with low-level
minor problems	subordinates
lack of preparation for	keeping up with former
meetings	position
correspondence delays	unclear job description
conflicting goals	interpersonal conflict
obsolete policies and	lack of performance
procedures	feedback

Such items are not unfamiliar to most managers. Everyone recognizes some of his personal enemies on this list.[1] Nonetheless, most of the factors are superficial; they represent symptoms, not causes. They also erroneously imply that anything that interferes with the way managers want to spend their time is wasteful. Doing what others want us to do may sometimes be more time-efficient than what we want to do. We need to examine the more fundamental time wasters: fractionated days, short-run perspectives, and fear of ambiguity.

Fractionated Days

Table 1 is a summary of how time is spent by the chief administrative assistant to a senior United States senator in Washington, D.C. On an average day he talks with more than twenty-five different people, which takes over 85 percent of his time. Most of these talks are initiated by others to whom he must respond. And the day is very jumpy. The average incident such as talking to someone lasts about two minutes. The average interval of quiet time alone is only five minutes!

Under such conditions, the A.A.'s day is devoted mainly to responding to various telephone calls, visitors, voters, and colleagues. His life is dominated by the present and by fight-

Table 1. Percentage of Time at Work Spent in Communication Activities by Administrative Assistant to U.S. Senator*

Activity	Total	Senator	Legislative Assts.	Exec. Secretary	Legislative Corresps. & Support Pers.	Field Staff	Non-office Pers.	Unknown
Oral communications	85%	35%	15%	<1%	2%	7%	15%	10%
Other-initiated	74	35	12	<1	2	6	14	4
telephone	18	<1	0	0	0	6	7	4
in person	56	35	12	<1	2	0	7	0
Self-initiated	11	0	3	0	<1	<1	1	6
telephone	11	0	3	0	<1	<1	1	6
in person	<1	0	0	0	<1	0	0	0
Reading & processing mail & memos	10							
Writing	5							

* Data based on observed behavior. Average length of communication: less than two minutes. Average interval of uninterrupted time: approximately five minutes.

ing immediate fires. The future shrinks in apparent importance because he has no time to deal with it.

Transition difficulty. Making transitions from shorter-term
emergencies to longer-run desirables is indeed difficult. One
day while I visited with this administrative assistant shortly
after lunch, there was a lull in the day's activities. Five
minutes, six minutes passed without an incident or a telephone call. As the minutes passed, he began to get nervous
—he was playing with his pencil, glancing at his watch, and
shuffling papers. At about the tenth uninterrupted minute
he said to me that this was the most difficult part of the day.

I asked him why, since he wasn't doing anything!

The aide pointed to a pile of papers and explained that
they were nominations from the White House for positions
in the State Department. Since his senator was a ranking
member of the Senate Foreign Relations Committee, he was
to write letters for the senator to the president commenting
on each of the nominees.

This was a ticklish assignment. Since the letters might
well become public, they had to be carefully drafted so as not
to offend political friends. The harried A.A. indicated he
couldn't bring himself to begin the tough thinking and writing because he expected to be interrupted any minute. Finally, he chose to put the letters into his brief case for
consideration later at home.

Perhaps it was proper time management for the senator's
assistant to take the creative work home (we shall consider
this later). Nonetheless, the moral of this tale is that the
present tends to tyrannize the future. Programmed and immediate tasks tend to be handled before more ambiguous
and longer-run matters.

Such tyranny of the present is not confined to government, of course. A study of high-level business executives
also revealed short intervals of uninterrupted time, insufficient for concentrated thought and contemplation.[2] The average span of time alone was fourteen minutes—and if

telephone calls were counted, the average period without interruption was only eight minutes.

Five or ten minutes alone are helpful only for work on small, immediate problems. They are unsuitable for long-range matters and even too short as rest intervals. Many executives in this study did not believe that they spent up to an hour and a half alone during the day. All they knew was that they scarcely had time to start a new task or light a cigarette or even take a good, deep breath before they were interrupted by the arrival of a visitor or the ringing of their telephone.

Too little thinking.   The result of continuing dominance by immediate demands is that one has inadequate time for reading and thinking. As a result managers tend to be narrow in their interests and concentrate on technical and economic reading.

Worst of all, time-harried people take insufficient time for internal exploration. Dominated by response behavior for long periods, they can lose track of who they are and what they believe. Losing touch with their own values and aspirations, they find it impossible to initiate fundamental changes. The future is never confronted.

A United States senator poignantly complained of the pressures of the present when he said, "The job gets you. You lose track of what is your real political philosophy. You start voting to maintain your image rather than what you really believe." This was a senator who as a young representative had started out very liberal in his views. He continued to vote liberal as he moved into middle age but felt increasingly uncomfortable with it. Only when he finally began to take time to examine bills in the light of his evolving beliefs did he begin to vote more as a conservative—to the consternation of his liberal staff and constituents. Perhaps Winston Churchill's famous observation applies here: "Anyone who is not a socialist at age twenty has no heart, but anyone who is not a conservative at forty has no brains!"

Short-run Time Perspectives

The famous economist John Maynard Keynes once responded to the conservatives' insistence that in the long run economic depression would cure itself through the free market with the acid comment: "In the long run, we're all dead." For Keynes, and for President Roosevelt eventually, saving private enterprise and democratic society were more important than preserving a certain model of capitalism. Perhaps they were right, perhaps not; the problem is that the manager cannot wait. Without action, failure looms.

Rewards and punishment. Politicians and government officials tend to concentrate on the short run because of threats in the near future: defeat of a bill, reduction of the yearly appropriation, rejection by the voters. Long-range demographic, agricultural, or environmental problems will not hurt them *now* (although they may not be able to say this much longer). In this short-range view, small matters bulk large.

Political history suggests that a manager needs one thing above all others to accomplish great and lasting things —time. Conquest and destruction can be completed quickly, but building takes longer. Consider the United States government's apparent repetition of so many of France's mistakes and even our own earlier errors in Southeast Asia. The sense of déjà vu is overwhelming when one looks at articles of twenty-five years ago. Writing in 1971 when our policy in Vietnam was collapsing, a Rand Corporation researcher commented:

> Through the years, the same strategies have been used with different names, but the same old mistakes have been made. Why have these mistakes been repeated? For one thing, there is a lack of institutional memory in the American organization in Vietnam. Any lessons learned here have not been transmitted to people who followed the people who learned the lessons. This is due primarily to the short tours of duty, the rapid turnover of people. The one-year tour—especially for people in command jobs or running programs—has been disastrous. A

person comes in, works hard for a year and then leaves, giving the job to someone else with no experience.[3]

Life and death are not as close to the business manager, of course, but dominance of present over future can be as great. Short-term performance standards encourage many managers to concentrate on the now. Frequently they feel that they are rewarded or punished for *this* year based upon short-run, objective measures of profits, costs, and growth. In the long run they will be dead—or transferred. A competitive business system encourages a short-time perspective, of course; only a monopoly can ignore the present. Yet, even given competiton, management tends to measure performance over too limited a time span. Concentration on the present is usually rewarded, while concern for the future is often punished.

Corporate rotation and transfer policies also contribute to the dominance of short-range time orientations. General Electric has a justified reputation as a well-managed company. Yet back in its most decentralized period in the 1960s operating managers would sometimes exploit equipment, people, and even customers to optimize performance in the short run. Equipment would not be maintained, employees would not be trained, and customer complaints not responded to in the hope that the department's results would look so good *this year* that the manager in charge would be rewarded with a promotion. His or her unsuspecting replacement would have to pick up the pieces.

In many growing firms, supermobile managers average a position change every eighteen months: even average managers move every two or three years.[4] Such transfers and short tenures do not reflect job mastery so much as they express impatience with progress up the hierarchy. Mobile managers tend to measure their success by how frequently they are promoted or transferred not by how well they perform. They never are afforded the luxury of failure or time to learn, so the first setback is catastrophic. This lends credence to Laurence Peter's *Peter Principle* that every managerial slot in hierarchical organizations is eventually filled with an incompetent because managers are promoted to the level of their incompetence.[5] This is an exaggeration, of course, because people can and do grow as they move upward, but the point is clear: our national culture, organizational climate, and personal attitudes emphasize the present.

Inadequate planning.   Managers with high achievement need desire feedback indicating they have performed effectively. But they tend to be impatient. They want results quickly, for that is the purpose of their effort and discipline. Unfortunately, excessive concern with rapid progress and feedback hinders progress. Too much attention is directed to the present, to the short-run payoff, without adequate concern for the future. In the effort to act now, managers fail to collect necessary information, to plan, and to think for the future.

Many observers suggest that this predilection toward action over thought is characteristic of American culture in general. Patience is an easy virtue when the prevailing cultural view of time is circular, with its infinite length and repetition. However, patience is difficult with a linear perspective. We are concerned about the future, but our future must be relatively close. Ours is not the distant future of the East, which is far beyond present influence; ours is just up the road a piece. Witness the situation in Indochina: for years we deluded ourselves that victory was around the bend, or that we saw the light at the end of the tunnel, or that it was the beginning of the end. Yet the enemy's time scale for accepting warfare and delaying victory was beyond ours. "While we look to the future," Edward Hall wrote, "our view of it is limited. The future to us is the foreseeable future, not the future of the South Asian that may involve centuries."[6] And that was written years before our military involvement in Vietnam.

Not thinking about the future may even stem from being successful in the present and confident about the future. The most pervasive theme in James MacGregor Burn's biography of Franklin Roosevelt is short-run ingenuity and tactical brilliance.[7] Apparently the very competence of the president to manage the turbulence about him led to enormous confidence that he could similarly manage the Soviet Union and postwar conditions. No real plan or philosophy was formulated to implement the confidence—and unfortunately FDR died.

Such conditions of competence in the present and perhaps overconfidence about being able to handle the future characterize many successful managers. Therefore they never find the time to consider the future. As former RCA chairman David Sarnoff suggested, "You know our brain needs exercise as well as our muscle. A great many people don't go beyond today. If things are going along all right today, they are not thinking about five, or ten, or twenty years from now."[8]

Not thinking about the future finds its most common form in inability to defer gratification. To lower forms of life, now is the only reality; needs must be satisfied immediately. Higher up, the intervals of gratification delay increase: we are told that a rat can sustain a delay of some four minutes; a cat, seven hours; a chimpanzee, forty-eight hours. In man the delay may reach beyond his own existence.

Of course, people vary. Children have short time-delay spans; it is difficult to postpone satisfaction because the future lacks much meaning to someone without much of a past. Immature persons act on the basis of immediate need without much anticipation of later, secondary consequences. High insurance rates for youthful drivers reflect not their ability (which is superior to older people) but their tendency to consider only the present when tearing along the highway heedless of possibilities around the bend.

What is attributed to youngsters is characteristic of most adults in some cultures, and of perhaps everyone everywhere under certain conditions. In countries whose ancient glories are celebrated as if they happened yesterday, businessmen have been known to invest large amounts in factories without making the slightest plan how to use them. In this case, the future seems unreal.

Lack of faith in the future.   The bird in the hand, the bridge to cross later, and the poet's "Ah, take the Cash, and let the Credit go, / Nor heed the rumble of a distant Drum" are all attractive to all people sometimes but hold special appeal to those who doubt what is in the bush, expect never to reach the bridge, or know from experience that promises tend to be broken—in short, those with parents, relatives, and friends for whom no other perspective has paid off.

Although such conditions frequently apply to the poor, there is no intrinsic connection between time orientation and lower class. Whenever people of any social class have been uncertain or downright pessimistic about the future, "I want mine right now" has been a common response. The stories of promiscuity during World War II at some colleges dwarf the tales about today's students. In times of stress all classes tend to throw off conventional restraints and appear less able to defer gratification; future time orientation appears to collapse in favor of the present.

There is a story about an American agricultural expert visiting in the United Arab Republic. The American asked a local farmer about his expected yield. The Arab was highly insulted since he thought the American considered him crazy. To the traditional Arab, only God knows the future and it is presumptuous even to talk about it. Perhaps the Egyptian farmer had faith, but planning requires even greater faith: the expenditure of time now is an investment in the future—and sometimes a risky investment. It assumes that tomorrow will come and that action today will make a difference.

People may not plan because they fail to think about the future or because they can conceive of nothing good there. Individually most managers are achievement-oriented, time-conscious, and mildly optimistic—at least to the extent of believing that action helps. Within organizations, however, ignoring the future is not rare.[9] Much talk is heard about the future in business and politics, but until recently the talk was preceded by little real thought—witness the reluctance to think about the implications of despoilment of the atmosphere, rivers, lakes, and oceans. Inability to delay gratification has certainly characterized American industrial development.

Fear of Ambiguity

Many managers focus on the present because the future is too ambiguous, hence threatening. Everyone has limited tolerance for ambiguity; we tend to prefer the known (especially if it is acceptable) to the unknown. We prefer the act that has measurable results to the intangible or unmeasurable. This leads managers to concentrate on details, about which then they complain so loudly.

Excessive attention to detail.   Every organization has an inexhaustible supply of detailed issues needing attention—*now!* "I waste my time on trivia," managers complain. "If I could get rid of such nonsense, I would spend my time on important planning and evaluating" is their plea. Perhaps they mean this, but many really want the demand for detailed activity. Managers are not forced to expend all their time on trivialities; the opposite may be true. The real challenges of managing are so difficult and anxiety-provoking that managers allow their days to be filled with detail and trivia. This protects them from having any time to contemplate what they are *not* doing. At least, when they issue a directive modifying travel allowances, they "accomplish" something tangible, real, and comforting.

A former chairman of Inland Steel writes about the self-appointed martyr that is the poor, harried, overworked manager: "Pity the overworked executive! Behind his paperwork ramparts, he struggles bravely with a seemingly superhuman load of responsibilities. Burdened with impossible assignments, beset by constant emergencies, he never has a chance to get organized. Pity him but recognize him for the dangerous liability that he is."[10]

This attention to familiar detail has special impact when a manager is promoted. Sometimes he continues to hold on to his former position through close supervision, partly because he lacks trust in his replacement, but mainly because he seeks the comfort of the familiar. Managers tend to concentrate on what they know they do well. Such behavior emphasizes the present at the expense of the future and the old to the detriment of the new.

Fear of losing control. Nowhere is this fear of ambiguity and its effect on time utilization more evident than in controlling subordinates. In collaborative or participative management the superior does not always know what his subordinate is doing—he knows only what the subordinate chooses to reveal. Collaborative leadership means that, for a time after the desired objectives have been agreed upon, the subordinate is free to explore his own means. For example, after superior and subordinate agree that the latter needs a cost-accounting and control system in his department, and the superior sets limits upon what can be spent in setting it up, he must give the subordinate freedom even though the superior may be an expert on such matters. The superior should live with ambiguity and allow his subordinate to suggest his own proposal. Why wait for this? Because the subordinate will probably make his own plan work more effectively *even if it is intrinsically inferior to an expert's.*

The superior should create an environment in which he is informed voluntarily, and he should refrain from probing for a reasonable time. The superior may be anxious, especially if his own boss is exerting pressure because his authoritarian concept of management requires him to know exactly what his subordinates are doing at all times. A manager needs courage to demonstrate collaborative leadership when his own superior is authoritarian.

Under threat from superiors and fear of ambiguity, many managers overcontrol. Consider the following example from a training session with state employees. Three hierarchical levels were present: the state director of correction, the deputy director in charge of prisons, and prison wardens. The deputy reiterated the old organization principle that responsibility cannot be delegated, that he would hold each warden personally responsible for anything the guards did wrong (from supplying a car for an escaping inmate to smuggling in forbidden copies of *Playboy*). The wardens were well aware that this attitude made their preceding discussion of delegation and decentralization irrelevant. The deputy director's dictum would require extensive monitoring of guards because the most effective way to control closely is to interject yourself between subordinates so that most communications pass through you. This may or may not be effective prison management (the wardens felt that it would have relatively little effect on whether or not a given guard would collaborate), but it certainly would consume time and sabotage decentralization.

The desire for control and certainty leads to some strange inversions of activities. In one small printing shop, customers coming in the front door were the life of the business. There was no sales staff; mail orders were not possible; and telephone orders were few. The person who opened the front door and jingled a little bell *was* the business. Yet the proprietor would be clearly annoyed by their arrival. He perceived customers as interruptions to his paperwork— completing jobs tickets, estimating, calculating, and so on. As much as managers complain about paperwork, it is tangible and controllable. They can start and stop as they please, take a drink of water when thirsty, speed up, or slow down. In contrast, the customer is not under control; he initiates the conversation and tries to persuade the manager to do what he wants. Of course, to serve the customer is the function of the business, but unconsciously a manager may prefer the known, the concrete, and the self-controlled.

Fear of ambiguity and of losing control also contributes to a crisis syndrome. Of course, legitimate crises created by the environment or technology can lead to effective performance and high morale (supposedly, many people enjoyed World War II—when they were not being shot at). For example, under pressure from President Kennedy to produce equipment to detect Soviet nuclear tests in the early 1960s, the Sandia Corporation was steeped in a crisis atmosphere. In a short time, it produced substantial technological innovations enabling the United States to agree to the atmospheric test ban treaty without inspection. This crisis was dramatic and clearly necessary; it gave direction and meaning to an organization.[11]

However, many crises are artificial, like the "Hurry up and wait" of military fame. Such fraudulent conditions seem to grow from the hierarchical structure itself. A high-level executive feels that a completion date is necessary to keep the organization on its toes; he assigns one that he thinks reasonable. Each subordinate manager wants to impress his superior so he advances the date a little. Thus time pressure increases as the deadline moves lower in the hierarchy, generating an arbitrary crisis that no one understands but that is a customary state in so many organizations.

Fear of not being in control and of being adrift in ambiguity contributes to the long hours of some managers. An oil company president complains, "I don't know why, but everybody around me works too hard. . . . My executive group all work too much. I think that's a bit characteristic of business executives in the United States today. If anything, they spend too many hours at work."[12]

CHAPTER 3
Making Lists

Like most time-haunted, action-oriented people you probably feel weighted down by lists. These range from "things to
do today" kept neatly on a daily or weekly calendar to those
crumpled memo notes that fill your pockets and go through
the wash with your shirts. Sometimes you feel enslaved by
such lists.

Like death and taxes, lists will always be with achieve-
ment-directed managers and professionals. Nonetheless
there are several approaches to lists that allow you to manage time more actively than by merely responding to items
listed as they arise.

Ivy Lee's $25,000 Advice

One of the oldest schemes found in time management literature is that of Ivy Lee, a management consultant, fifty
years ago.[1] Lee was having dinner with Charles Schwab,
then chairman of Bethlehem Steel Company. Schwab complained of the many things he had to do and wished that Lee
could give him some good advice on time management. The
resourceful Lee thereupon wrote out the following on the
back of the menu:

- Every evening . . .
    write down the six most important tasks for tomorrow in
    order of priority.
- Every morning . . .
    start working on item one and continue until you finish
    it; then start on item two, and so on.
- At end of day . . .
    tear up list—and start over!

Schwab asked Lee how much he wanted for the advice, but
the consultant told the executive to use the plan for several
weeks before paying him whatever Schwab thought it was
worth. Lee eventually received a check for $25,000 (approx-
imately $100,000 in today's money!).

The advice appears to be simplicity itself. Especially attractive is the idea of tearing up last night's list at the end of the day whether or not you have completed all the tasks. Drawing up a new list for tomorrow will demand that you reexamine your tasks and priorities in terms of the present situation.

Unfortunately the Lee advice has a glaring weakness that renders it of marginal usefulness. It assumes that the list maker controls all of his or her time. No equipment breakdowns, uncertain subordinates, insistent customers, or rapacious competitors would seem to interfere with the manager serenely moving down the list.

But this is an unreasonable assumption about an unrealistic world. No manager can control all of his time. No executive can single-mindedly proceed down her list of tasks. Perhaps only a very independent worker like a tenured college professor could do so. Former college professor Henry Kissinger was asked shortly after he left the post of secretary of state to contrast academic life with service in the White House. Kissinger replied that as a professor he could generally follow the priority list approach—that is, list the book he wanted to work on, the article to be revised, the course curriculum to be developed, the committee meeting to be held. Then he could generally proceed down the list. When he came into the White House, he tried to utilize the same technique. He would bring his list into 1600 Pennsylvania Avenue on Monday morning at 7:00 A.M. and begin. Unfortunately, at 7:15 A.M. there would be a revolution in some obscure part of the world and the rest of the day and week would be shot to pieces![2]

Less dramatically, virtually all managers or professionals working in organizations are subject to routine interruptions and unforeseen emergencies. You cannot entirely escape them nor should you necessarily try if, like Kissinger discovered, responding to them is and should be a central aspect of your job.

However unrealistic as primary time management advice, Ivy Lee's priority list approach can be useful *as part of* some other approaches to be discussed.

Edwin Bliss's 80–20 Rule

Edward Bliss offers a variant of the Ivy Lee list.[3]

- Each evening draw up your "to do" list of ten desirable activities (those you will probably not get to under the pressure of tomorrow's demands unless you fight for time).
- Schedule blocks of tomorrow's time for the two highest priority activities on the list.
- Perform the two activities in the scheduled time. If you complete them and discretionary time is still available, move on to the other activities from last night's list.

This approach asserts the so-called 80–20 rule from statistics, namely, that 80 percent of the total variance in a population of people or items is caused by just 20 percent. For example, employers find that 80 percent of their absenteeism occurs among only some 20 percent of their employees; or that 20 percent of a firm's product line produces 80 percent of the total profits. The principle is certainly not universal, but the 80–20 relationship loosely applies in many circumstances.

Thus Bliss assumes that 80 percent of the total importance in a "to do" list is contained in just 20 percent of the items. Completing two activities out of a list of ten will accomplish 80 percent of what was truly important (one hopes). A virtue of this approach is modesty in a manager's expectations. That is, you shouldn't feel defeated if unable to accomplish all the items on a current list.

Joseph Trickett's Activity Analysis

This activity analysis begins with a single list that is then divided and analyzed in four ways.[4] Therefore you will need five sheets of paper headed as indicated in Figure 1.

List of activities.   List all of the recurring activities that characterize your job. It might include such things as answering mail inquiries, checking product quality, counseling subor-

Figure 1.   Joseph Trickett's Activity Analysis

1.   List of Activities in My Job

2.   Activity Analysis — Intrinsic Importance

Very Important, must be done	Important, should be done	Not So Important, may not be necessary but may be useful	Unimportant, can be eliminated

3.   Activity Analysis — Urgency

Very Urgent, must be done now	Urgent, should be done soon	Not Urgent, long-range	Time Not a Factor

4.   Activity Analysis — Delegation

Must be done by me	Can be delegated to A	Can be delegated to B	Can be delegated to C	Can be delegated to D	Can be delegated to E

5.   Activity Analysis — Communications

People I must see every day	People to see frequently	People to see regularly	People to see only infrequently

dinates, tracking down lost parts, planning the budget, and so on. Don't list them according to priorities, but write them down in any way that ensures that the list is inclusive. Include both routine and at least predictable types of emergencies. This should require approximately fifteen minutes. This list of activities will be the basic working document that you will subject to the various analyses.

Activity analysis for intrinsic importance.   The second sheet of paper should contain four columns: (1) very important, must be done; (2) important, should be done; (3) not so important, may not be necessary but could be useful; and (4) unimportant, can be eliminated.

Now take all of the activities listed on your first sheet and parcel them out under the four columns on this second sheet, called activity analysis for intrinsic importance. "Intrinsic importance" is a subjective concept, but it reflects your best judgment as to the activities' contribution to accomplishing the firm's objectives. Remember, each activity should appear in only one column. They should *not* all be listed in the left-hand, "very important" column (and most of you may find it difficult to put any of your activities in the right-hand column, "unimportant, can be eliminated"). When the intrinsic importance analysis is completed, put this second sheet aside.

Activity analysis for urgency.   This third sheet of paper should also contain four columns: (1) very urgent, must be done now; (2) urgent, should be done soon; (3) not urgent, long-range; and (4) time not a factor. These categories reflect how quickly after a "cue" the activity must be performed; immediately, fairly soon, or anytime. For example, you are a production manager sitting at your desk analyzing last week's output figures, when all of a sudden you hear a loud grinding noise coming from your assembly line. You immediately rush out of your office to check what has gone awry. Such checking should be done immediately after the cue, hence "very urgent, must be done now."

Once again, ensure that every activity listed on your first sheet is parceled out in one of the four columns on this third sheet, activity analysis for urgency.

Activity analysis for delegation. Before actually filling out this fourth sheet of paper, Trickett suggests, you should compare your second and third sheets. That is, put your "activity analysis for intrinsic importance" next to your "activity analysis for urgency." He maintains that there will be very few activities in both left hand columns of the analyses. That is, few activities will be "very important" *and* "very urgent." For the most part, he argues, important activities are not urgent. Similarly, urgent activities will seldom be of great intrinsic importance—or so Trickett suggests.

President Eisenhower is reported to have conducted such an analysis early in his first term when he felt overloaded by staff pressures to make decisions more rapidly.[5] Ike concluded that most of the matters that his staff considered urgent were actually of minor importance. The really big and important issues in his opinion tended to have substantial time for analysis and decision.

This comparison of importance and urgency sets the stage for the third analysis—activity analysis for delegation. This fourth sheet of paper should have a column for yourself, "must be done by me," and separate columns for each of your immediate subordinates to whom you might delegate activities. Each of the activities should be parceled out among the columns on this sheet. Trickett's advice on delegation is essentially as follows:

- Assign the relatively few very important *and* very urgent activities to yourself. That is, list them in the left hand column, "must be done by me."
- Assign the very important but not urgent activities also to yourself.
- Delegate the urgent but not so important activities to your subordinates according to a continuum beginning with relatively more important and less urgent matters to the most

competent subordinate and ending with urgent and less important activities to the least competent or least experienced subordinate.

What Trickett's approach attempts to do is to free you from the dominance of present urgent but less important demands. This should allow you to devote time to longer-range and fundamentally more important matters. This is the approach Eisenhower tried to take. Of course, not everyone admires President Eisenhower's style or performance! Some feel he was too passive in not confronting urgent issues. Others criticize him for allowing his staff in effect to run the government because he was aloof from urgent problems.

Still, the Eisenhower White House had a serenity about it in sharp contrast to his immediate predecessors and successors. In his criticism of the Kennedy and Johnson administrations' handling of the Vietnam war, the generally liberal reporter David Halberstam almost grudgingly praises Eisenhower for knowing when "not making a decision" or saying no was the proper action.[6] Presidents Kennedy and Johnson were perhaps too confident of the White House's ability to manage all important, urgent, and in-between matters.

The key assumption in the Trickett approach is that urgency and importance do not generally march together. Therefore, few managers will be overloaded strictly with important *and* urgent matters. To the extent that this assumption is not valid for your job, this approach loses its value.

Activity analysis for communication.   The most attractive part of the Trickett method may be this fourth analysis, which contains four columns: (1) people I must talk to every day; (2) people to talk to frequently; (3) people to talk to regularly; and (4) people to talk to only infrequently.

Go back to your first sheet of paper, your activities list, and write down the people you communicate with in performing the activities. Each activity should have a name or names associated with it. These names, not the activities, are the working data for this fourth analysis. Allocate all of the names across the columns on the activity analysis for communications.

The communications analysis allows you to maintain a separate agenda for personal contacts. Initiation of talks with appropriate people should go on your daily "to do" lists along with activities. This separate agenda is to prevent urgent activities from totally determining who you talk to in any given time period. It will encourage you to make time to tend to your interpersonal relationships (a fancy term for office politics). Such politicking is not necessarily Machiavellian power tactics. It is mainly good human relations. When you need another manager's advice in an emergency, it helps when you have already set up a personal, friendly relation with that person. It assures you of immediate attention when it is most needed.

When I first started out in a corporate staff position along with other young industrial engineers, we were each assigned an office and a telephone. We hung our framed credentials on the wall. The more naïve among us then waited for the phone to ring, waited for operating managers to solicit our expertise. We were soon disabused of this notion— or we became lonely at our silent desks.

What was needed, we discovered, was to "sell ourselves" to the line managers. This meant traveling out to the plant, developing relationships, and tending to them. I was struck by how the more energetic young staff advisers maintained lists of who they wanted to talk to, what hobbies the manager pursued, and what job problems particularly interested them. It was not a catch-as-catch-can matter but a Trickettlike program.

When Lyndon Johnson entered the United States Senate as a freshman senator from Texas, he would leave his office up to ten times a day to go to the lavatory. Rather than use his own private facility, he would walk around the building and even to other floors. His biographer tells us that these rambles were not random.[7] They faciliated his meeting other people "accidentally on purpose." Senate mores discourage a senator from asking other senators directly how they are going to vote, but Johnson's chance encounters with august members of the Senate establishment such as Richard Russell of Georgia enabled him to develop links and pick up information.

This is precisely what Trickett's fourth analysis is designed to promote. A report on the early career experiences of young M.B.A. graduates suggests that this is one of the sharpest differences between those who are more and those who are less successful.[8] The less successful passively allow their narrow tasks to determine what they learn and who they communicate with. In contrast, the more effective workers actively explore the organization by developing and maintaining relationships with a wider variety of people.

Such interpersonal behavior may appear to be wasteful of time in the short run, but it clearly is a wise investment in the future.

CHAPTER 4

Keeping Logs and Diaries

"Here's your day: 9-10, doodling; 10-11, on hold; 11-12, tidy desk; 12-2, lunch; 2-3, paper shuffling; 3-4, woolgathering; 4-5, clock watching; 5, head home."

Peter Drucker recommends that, rather than analyzing activity lists drawn from memory, you collect actual data on where your time goes.[1] These data can be analyzed and used to change behavior if desired.

Peter Drucker's Diary

For a couple of weeks you should maintain a chronological record of what you do to generate the basic working data for your analysis. The format of the diary is not important, but entries should be frequent, as soon as an activity occurs if possible. Don't wait until lunch time to write down everything you did in the morning. You won't remember. If feasible, a parallel record of your activities kept by a secretary would be valuable.

Three pertinent questions.   Drucker suggests that you review the scenario of your work life and subject it to three questions.

  • What does not have to be done?
  • What could be done by someone else?
  • What do I do that wastes the time of others?

Drucker recommends that you examine each diary entry initially to see if the activity could be eliminated. That is, when the cue presented itself or when the thought occurred to you, could it have been ignored without cost to the organization?

Such judgment is not easy, of course. The ability to make such decisions is at the core of Drucker's definition of the effective manager. To Drucker, a manager is a person who is able to transcend the flow of current events, to project him- or herself above the present and visualize past and future. From this perspective he or she can distinguish the important from the unimportant, the fundamental from the trivial.

From such an admittedly intuitive analysis, the effective

manager may be able to detect those activities that should be eliminated and those cues that can be safely ignored at minimal cost.

What this means is that everything doesn't have to be done, that perfect quality or "zero defects" is not always desirable. Implicit in Drucker's approach is that it is sometimes more managerial (and more efficient) to settle for less. For example, a manufacturing firm purchases waste material from various suppliers. It pays by the pound and the suppliers mark the number of pounds on each container. Because of variety in the material and containers, the weight per container varies widely. To check on the amount purchased, the firm weighs every container even though the supplier weighed it. Individual boxes sometimes differ in the two weighings, but no significant discrepancies exist over time. The managerial perspective according to Drucker suggests that individually weighing all those containers is silly and wasteful of time. Either accept the supplier's figures or periodically sample the weights to detect systematic cheating. The little amount you may overpay will be more than compensated by the time and cost savings at your end.

Excessively conscientious people intolerant of ambiguity will have difficulty in judging any behavior as unnecessary.

Central to the Drucker managerial model (along with distinguishing the necessary from the unnecessary) is converting crisis to routine. By examining the flow of events, an effective manager can detect the predictable crises that can be converted to routine by anticipating them through standing policies and procedures. When the incident occurs, it need not be handled as a unique problem. Rather it has been analyzed in advance and remedies are available.

On board a United States Navy ship, responses to the predictable emergencies are rehearsed to convert them to routine. Thus on a destroyer during every four-hour shift, the whole watch crew will rehearse responses to such crises as loss of steering control, detecting an unidentified submarine, losing electrical power, and so on. Similarly, a business could define procedures to be followed for predictable crises such as an intoxicated employee, wildcat strike, plant accident, or impending loss of a major customer.

Most readers probably feel that this Drucker perspective is obvious to managers. The need to anticipate is all-important in management. Many, many nonmanagers do not think this way, however. Professionals such as physicians and attorneys, for example, are inclined to take each case as unique, to focus full attention and analysis on it. The moral and professional advantages of such an approach are evident, but it consumes much time. My experience as observer of United States senator offices suggests that this is the predominant orientation. Events are handled as unique, priorities are not differentiated, and crisis predominates.

What professionals and politicians fear about converting crisis to routine is that events will be assigned to the wrong categories, that something truly unique and important will be treated as routine. The subtly different symptoms of the rare disease will be undetected and the patient mistakenly treated for a familiar illness. The letter from an especially influential constituent will be handled by a junior aide who orders up a reply of computer-stored paragraphs.

If a job truly contains no predictable crises because every event is unique, then it really cannot be managed according to the Drucker philososphy. Such a job can be handled only in a craft or professional mode as a series of discrete events.

Two delegation guidelines. Assuming that your diary analysis reveals some predictable patterns (not everything is unique), Drucker suggests two guidelines for delegating.

1. Keep the unique; delegate the routine. If a manager has been able to convert most crises to routine, administration of the response policies and procedures can be assigned to subordinates. Thus, Drucker argues, the manager will have time to concentrate on the truly important, unique problems and crises. This is the classic "management by exception" principle: subordinates handle the predictable; the superior focuses on the exceptional.

In theory, the exception principle is attractive. In practice, it is often impossible to distinguish between fundamental and trivial exceptions. As a result, the manure can flow upward instead of downward. The superior may get everything that is not specifically assigned to someone else.

2. Keep the activities in which you enjoy the greatest differential advantages (up to your time limit and energy capacity); delegate the activities in which you enjoy the least advantage. And, of course, delegate those that you handle less effectively than others. You should compare your own performance of each major activity with that of each available subordinate. As Figure 2 indicates, in some activities you will enjoy a large advantage; on others it will be small.

Distinguishing between the exceptional and the routine is easy to conceive, but "diffferential advantage" is tougher. The easiest situation to visualize is when you are truly superior. You can do every task in your unit better than any of your subordinates. You have the training, expertise, and ex-

Figure 2. Peter Drucker's Concept of Delegation Based on Differential Advantage

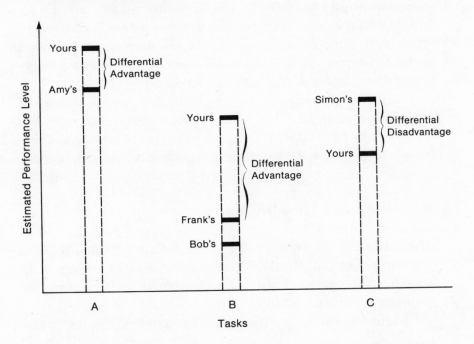

perience to be literally the best person for everything! But you can't do everything yourself (and live very long). You must delegate.

Note that this delegation guideline means that you may not concentrate on those things that you do best and enjoy most. You may delegate your best activities because you do them only marginally better than a subordinate. You may not be as good at other tasks, but you are still much better than your subordinates. For example, task A in Figure 2 is your best in absolute performance, but you are only slightly better than one of your subordinates. You would be wise to delegate task A to her. You are not as good on task B as on A, but you are far superior to Bob and Frank. You will want to keep task B even though it is not your best or favorite. Finally, you will delegate task C because you are poorer on it than Simon.

There are several practical difficulties with this approach. First is the difficulty of accurately judging the performance of subordinates on tasks which they may never have done. And if they are understandably poor now, do they have the ability to improve, and to what level compared with you? Second is the difficulty of being honest with yourself in gauging your performance levels on various tasks. And third, will you actually have the courage to delegate those you do best to focus on those you do poorly?

Drucker also suggests methods, built upon the diary and delegation analysis, by which a manager's discretionary time can be expanded. We shall discuss this in the next chapter, but first we need to examine another time-log approach.

Alec Mackenzie's Time Inventory

If Drucker is the grand guru of time management, R. Alec Mackenzie is a faithful follower of the master.[2] Mackenzie expands the two-week diary into a permanent technique for monitoring and scheduling time.

Figure 3 illustrates the form Mackenzie suggests. It is a

Figure 3. Alec Mackenzie's Executive Time Inventory

Daily Goals	Mon. 1. 2. 3. 4. 5.	C A T E G O R Y #	Tues. 1. 2. 3. 4. 5.	C A T E G O R Y #	Wed. 1. 2. 3. 4. 5.	C A T E G O R Y #	Thurs. 1. 2. 3. 4. 5.	C A T E G O R Y #	Fri. 1. 2. 3. 4. 5.	C A T E G O R Y #	
9:00											
9:30											
10:00											
3:30											
4:00											
4:30											
5:00											

Allocation Category	%	Time Spent	% of Day	Time Spent	% of Day	Time Spent	% of Day	Time Spent	% of Day	Time Spent	% of Day	Summary Total Time	% of Week
1.													
2.													
3.													
4.													
5.													
6.													
7.													
8.													
Estimate of Effect.													

weekly form to be used continually. At first sight it appears quite complex, but you can use it by following a sequence of simple steps: (1) estimate your ideal allocation; (2) collect and summarize your actual time expenditure; and (3) modify discrepancies by setting daily time goals.

Ideal time allocation.   You begin filling out the form in the lower left-hand corner, in the box labeled "Allocation." Under "Category" you should list the major responsibilities of your job. These categories may be more or less than the eight lines allowed (you may have to modify the form), but the categories are larger than Joseph Trickett's "activities" discussed earlier. The list might include such broad categories as: monitoring departmental performance, evaluating individuals, training subordinates, planning the next budget, keeping up with market conditions, maintaining relations with customers.

After completing the list of responsibility categories, you should define your ideal time allocation among them. If you could control all of your time on the job, how would you like to spend it? You may have to pick these targets out of the air, but state them anyway. Perhaps you feel you should spend 20 percent of your time in developing subordinates, 10 percent talking to customers, 25 percent monitoring current performance, and so on. Incidentally, there is no "ideal" time allocation that applies to all managers. *You* must define what is best for you.

Actual time expenditure.   Now use the form as a Drucker-type diary to collect data on where your time is actually going. Ignore the "Daily Goals" section for a couple of weeks and just keep a record of activities and times. At the end of each day, tabulate the time actually devoted to each responsibility category and calculate the percentage.

You will of course uncover discrepancies each day between your actual and ideal, but don't worry about them, and don't try to correct them—yet. At the end of the week, summarize the total time and percentage distribution. After a couple of weeks of just collecting data and summarizing them, you should be in a position to decide whether you want to act.

Setting time goals. Clearly, Mackenzie's approach forces you to confront reality and to make some decisions. Do you really want to put your behavior where your mouth is? Do you really want to modify your actual time expenditure so that it is closer to what you say is ideal? His approach forces you to face these issues weekly and daily.

The "Daily Goals" section at the top of the form is to assist you in narrowing the discrepancies between actual and ideal. The daily goals thus are less results to be achieved than different activities to spend time on. Thus daily goals might include : (1) spend one hour telephoning old customers; (2) be available in my office for two hours to answer any questions subordinates might have; (3) find two hours to begin work on next year's budget; and so on. You could mark out the periods when you will try to do these activities, say 4:00–5:00 P.M. for the telephoning, 10:00 A.M. to 12:00 noon for subordinates, and 9:00–10:00 A.M. and 1:00–2:00 P.M. for the budget.

Mackenzie's executive time inventory looks frightening to most managers. They worry about how much time they must expend just to keep track of how their time is being expended! It is a little like money: to earn some you've got to spend some. To plan and control your time more effectively requires investing some time. The system probably requires about two hours per week.

Other users complain about the more practical matters of tabulating daily time expenditures and assigning them to categories. A manager's day comes in bits and pieces not neatly boxed segments: a minute on this, twenty seconds on that, an hour's conference. And within each time slot, multiple topics are discussed. A subordinate comes in to ask a question on quality control; his boss responds, but takes the opportunity to ask about next year's budget and to give some candid feedback about last week's output. All of this can be difficult to record on the inventory and more difficult to disentangle for summarizing.

Nonetheless, the great virtue of the Mackenzie approach is that it forces you to face your time allocation, indeed to become immersed in it so that you will be motivated to try and do something about it. Mackenzie has also advanced valuable recommendations for saving time and we shall discuss these in the next chapter along with parallel ones from Drucker.

CHAPTER 5

Expanding Discretionary Time

"What a day! Eleven busy signals, nine answering services and ten
recorded announcements!"

Long ago François Rabelais wrote: "How shall I be able to rule over others if I have not full power and command of myself?" This view underlies the contention that managers must actively control as much of their time as possible. Implied is that you are not really a manager if you let the job rule you instead of the reverse. If you let events determine fully what you do, your ability, knowledge, and position will slip away because you are too busy "operating." Accordingly, you should distinguish between two kinds of time: [1]

1. On the one hand there is time that is not under control— variously termed uncontrollable time, job-imposed time, required time, fixed time, and response time. The last term is most appropriate because this is the time consumed responding to events and to people with their requests, demands, and problems.
2. On the other hand there is the time you can control—called controllable time, self-imposed time, disposable time, and discretionary time. Again, the last term is most appropriate.

Peter Drucker suggests that no manager has more than 25 percent of his time under his control.[2] Others indicate that the controllability factor may run from 20 to 50 percent. Regardless of what the exact figure is, most advisers contend that it should be larger. An American Management Association publication maintains that the difference between effective and ineffective executives lies in the number, significance, and rate of completion of their discretionary tasks, not in how well they perform during response time.[3] As will be discussed later, we take exception to this downgrading of response time; it is important. All managers have on obligation to be available to their superiors, peers, and subordinates. But not all the time.

The central message of most advice on time management is to separate controllable from uncontrollable time and consolidate discretionary activities in controllable time. Simple as this message appears, it is difficult to implement because the tactic incurs costs as well as benefits.

Using Discretionary Time

For most managers the biggest problem with discretionary time is that it is so chopped up that it virtually disappears or becomes unusable. As noted in Chapter 2, events may occur every five to ten minutes on the average. Managers may underestimate how much discretionary time they potentially possess or find it impossible to start anything substantial for fear of being interrupted.

To use discretionary time and progress on a discretionary project you need time periods long enough for concentration. The minimum usable time span required by most people to really focus on a complex issue is one and a half to two hours.

Insulation.   Insulation consists of buffering the manager from organizational demands for limited time periods. The most common device is scanning and sorting incoming communications, of which a classic illustration is the United States presidency. By executive order in 1939, Franklin D. Roosevelt created the Executive Office of the President "to protect the President's time" by "excluding any matter that can be settled elsewhere."[4] This mechanism evolved into a group of assistants and counselors who stand between the president and almost all incoming communications. These people decide (1) *what* should be brought to the President's attention; (2) *who* should do it; (3) *how* it should be done; and (4) *when* it should be done.

In addition to controlling incoming communications, these assistants can also organize them by grouping conferences in specific periods of the day. Such grouping also gives the president more of a block of time to prepare for meetings.

Of course, most managers do not have such an elaborate staff. To gain similar benefits from an insulating buffer, they must depend upon an assistant or a secretary that does more than type and answer the phone. A competent aide should have enough discretion to redirect about half of a manager's incoming messages to more appropriate people. On matters that should reach the manager, an astute subordinate can anticipate his needs and save time by gathering relevant data and preparing preliminary suggestions. The intent of such activity is to ensure that the manager reads each incoming communication only once before a reply is drafted.

Using a buffer to limit access and interruptions is widespread. It defends the executive against those who would manipulate his time to their own interests. Yet for all its substantial benefits, the buffer mechanism has unfortunate defects. With the United States presidency, buffering has been criticized as dangerous. The assistants may insulate the president from information they consider trivial but that may be really important. The information reaching the president may be so filtered and biased that he is out of touch with reality. Former vice-president Hubert Humphrey once commented that he never perceived the magnitude of anti–Vietnam war feeling until he left office. And former White House press secretary George Reedy argues in *The Twilight of the Presidency* that the problem of keeping a chief executive in touch with reality is so severe that it poses a danger to the future of our country.[5] Reedy maintains that the White House is enveloped in a "velvet cocoon." Clark Clifford, former secretary of defense and a perennial adviser to Democratic administrations, remembers an Eisenhower aide telling him that Ike was spared night work because his staff boiled down 150-page memoranda to two pages. Clifford replied, "There is only one trouble. If I could be the fellow who prepares the two-page memo, I'd be President instead of Ike."[6]

Similarly, if less dramatically, every executive runs the risk of being isolated from his organization. Clarence Randall, former chairman of Inland Steel, writes about the loneliness and isolation of his post in his *Folklore of Management,* in which he disparages the stereotype of the president as being on top of every issue in his corporation.[7] Many managers fear compounding this problem by overly rigorous buffering by a zealous subordinate.

The maverick former Avis president Robert Townsend describes how he dealt with this decisively: he fired his secretary.[8] To control incoming calls, he simply informed the switchboard to connect calls only between 11:00 and 12:00 in the morning and 4:00 and 5:00 in the afternoon. At other times, they were to take names and indicate that the president would call back. Of course this practice introduces a time delay, but Townsend maintains that few matters are urgent within four hours. The practice also groups all telephone communications into small portions of the day. In addition, without a secretary no one sits outside the president's office blocking entry. Without this buffer, perhaps this chief executive can promote closer relations with his subordinates by ensuring that everyone gains access, not just the most energetic and aggressive subordinates.

Still, operating without any buffer seems extreme. More modestly, another company's entire management group agreed to shut down telephones for one hour in the morning, instructing the switchboard operator to take messages during that period rather than putting through any incoming calls.

Isolation. The most definite form of separation is physical isolation from the normal workplace. Across the street from the White House in the Executive Building, President Nixon had a small private office where he could work alone.[9] All presidents have found it essential to have secluded retreats as in Hyde Park, Key West, and Camp David. Business executives may also maintain two offices (an entrepreneur in Fairfield County, Connecticut, erected an office building intended specifically to provide second offices for Manhattan executives residing in Connecticut), but more common practices are to work at home one day a week, close the office door and refuse all calls, or merely to use travel time. "You don't have to talk to anybody on a plane," comments a company president. "A couple of hours on a plane and you can do a tremendous amount of concentration, and that's impossible in the office. You have to do it at home or under other conditions."

What is involved here is an effort to consolidate chunks

of uninterrupted time in order to think more deeply about organizational problems. Drucker tells of a bank executive who maintains that, for ninety minutes, "my secretary has strict instructions not to put anyone through except the president of the United States and my wife. The president very rarely calls and my wife knows better."

At the most modest level, a manager may gain a little isolation by refusing to participate in one of the most insistent demands, the working luncheon meeting. There he eats into his free time on an expense account at a lower rate of remuneration than he receives for his office time. Instead of thus working for their lunch money, some executives eat alone in the office, sit in the park, or go to the zoo. (Medical research supports skipping the working lunch in favor of eating alone because the working lunch is one of the most stressful executive activities.)[10]

Note that partial isolation does not mean postponing routine or boring tasks to the evening. Sometimes managers must take work home, of course, but putting things off until evening is often more procrastination than time management; it enables them to avoid organizing their time during the day.

Periodic isolation seems so simple, but risks are involved. Can the manager afford to be unreachable? The president of the United States clearly cannot, but many managers take much the same view of themselves. If they are accessible, how can they confine interruptions only to true emergencies? Who determines what is urgent?

Decisions about withdrawal frequency and length will depend upon position demands, the magnitude of potential emergencies, and faith in subordinates. An operating supervisor can be out of touch for only short periods; the demands of his technology and subordinates are too insistent, too quick-paced. A high-level general executive will have much more leeway.

Any withdrawal may create personal animosity. The associate or subordinate who calls with a matter that is important to him may be offended when he is denied entry. Even tougher, courage is required to withdraw from a superior's initiations for *any* length of time. He may expect his subordinate to be always on tap. In addition, the culture of the institution may discourage periodic withdrawal. At a meeting of church officials, one bishop maintained that withdrawal was simply impossible. The human values implicit in his religion's mission so permeate church administration that the administrator is expected to be a shepherd and servant to his associates and subordinates. The value system requires that he is available, understanding, and responsive. This may well hinder the performance of the institution because immediate problems will tend to dominate. Even in business some managers are afraid to close their doors—a closed door may suggest that some secret changes are being plotted; they can no longer say that "my door is always open"; the boss may think they are asleep.

Superiors should recognize their subordinates' problems in this regard. Managers rarely are sensitive about their responsibility to protect their subordinates' time for thinking, thereby contributing to the impulse to act at the expense of thought. Young managers particularly are caught in a bind between reflection and production. A superior should protect his subordinates by requiring thinking time and refusing to let them equate busywork with deliberation.

Some managers fear isolation and withdrawal because of their own personalities. Perhaps they fear the ambiguity of such periods; perhaps to maintain their drive, they must be on their feet talking with others; perhaps they fear time for thought because they have no idea what to think about.

Reserving blocks of time. Two-hour chunks are tough to carve out of most weeks. You will really have to fight to schedule them and then to preserve them from interruption. Techniques like insulation and isolation may help, but more fundamental is an awareness of the need to plan on a weekly basis for those periods when you will escape from the pressure of present demands and focus on longer-run discretionary concerns.

To facilitate scheduling discretionary blocks, some offices have experimented with "quiet hours." In a crowded office with many visitors, telephone calls, and conversations it just may be too noisy even for a self-disciplined scheduler really to concentrate during his or her discretionary time. A quiet hour is a period during which (1) all incoming telephone calls are blocked by a switchboard with a promise that the desired person will return the call at a certain time; (2) no visitors are scheduled; (3) no outgoing telephone calls are initiated; and (4) internal office communications or meetings are discouraged.

Such a system literally creates quiet in what can be a very noisy office. Because their office spaces are so crowded (much more so than in most business offices), some senators' staffs have instituted quiet hours two or three times a week to facilitate drafting letters, speeches, and bills that require concentrated thought and creativity.

Concentrating during discretionary time.   There are two kinds of people: sequential people and simultaneous people. Sequential people can focus on only one issue at a time, moving from the first to the second as they complete the task or push it along as far as it can go at the moment. Simultaneous people, however, are able to switch from one problem to the next and the next and back to the first problem without becoming harried in the process.

If you are going to be successful as a manager, you have to become a simultaneous person. Most of a manager's time is devoted to responding to various matters and these come simultaneously or very closely together. Unless you have the flexibility to switch rapidly from issue to issue, you are unlikely to be happy or effective as a manager. It would be better if you were an independent professional who enjoys greater control of his or her day.

So in response time you will need to be simultaneous. Discretionary time is different, however. Here you should be sequential. That is, you should focus on relatively few discretionary projects during your reserved blocks of time. Don't expect to move ahead on ten different projects during a ninety-minute chunk. To attempt to do so will only fractionate your time and attention as happens in response time. Transitions from topic to topic will likely be inefficient and your thinking murky.

Protecting prime time. "Prime time" is that time of the day when you are most alive and firing on all cylinders. It is the period of the day or week when you are most able to concentrate and be creative. Such time is especially precious.

Humans are creatures of cycles and most of us are fairly consistent in the periods that are our personal prime times. Some of us are "morning people" and can think most clearly from 6:00 to 9:00 A.M. Others are "night people" whose brains begin to percolate only with the moon. There is no necessary advantage in being either one or another. What is important, however, is to protect your personal prime time.

Discretionary time and projects should be scheduled in personal prime time, if possible. Thus you will be handling the most difficult and ambiguous problem solving during your most effective periods. The corollary is not to allow your prime time to be chewed up by routine problems. It is better to handle those when you are not at your absolute peak.

Thus it is probably silly for a morning type manager to devote his mornings to answering the mail, especially if the mail deals mainly with routine matters requiring little original thought. It is better to do this late in the afternoon when he or she is running low on energy and to reserve the morning for more difficult matters. Similarly, in my own work as a professor, I feel it is wasteful to expend my prime time on grading students' papers. I save them until the evening after dinner, perhaps reading them while sitting with my family watching (or more exactly, listening to) television. It is not that I do a better job of grading them than I would do in my prime time. I probably would grade better in the morning. Rather it is a judgment of comparative advantage. My discretionary type research and writing projects are done far better in morning prime time than in the afternoon or evening, whereas paper grading in the evening is only a little poorer than during prime time.

Concentrating discretionary projects in personal prime time is of course easier said than done! It depends somewhat on where your prime time is on the daily or weekly clock. If your prime time is early morning or late at night, you enjoy an advantage because others' demands are much lower at those times. If your prime time is a prosaic 9:00 A.M. to noon every day, you will have much more difficulty reserving discretionary blocks of time during prime time. Others just expect you to be available to respond during this time.

Using tidbits of time.   Unexpected empty time can be a curse or a blessing. If we have nothing to do we may fight our anxiety as we hear the clock tick away. If we are prepared to do something, these tidbits can be a gift.

Tidbits of time are available in a variety of ways: you have a scheduled meeting, but the other person is late; you have to sit in the reception area much longer than expected; on a field trip you find a whole afternoon free because some meetings were canceled; or an airline "equipment problem" gives you three hours to kill in an airport.

These gifts of time can be used if you are prepared with material to work with. One of the most effective time users I've ever met always carries his briefcase containing three kinds of folders:

- Manila folders containing current, response type items such as letters to be answered, production data to be checked, a rough draft of a report to be proofread and approved
- Pink folders containing discretionary projects currently being worked on, such as a tentative budget for next year, a new policy and procedure on individual performance evaluation, industry journals on new technical developments
- Blue folders for notes on future, "blue sky" possibilities; when a bright idea strikes, it is written down and filed in a blue folder

When the manager is feeling in peak form he may peruse the ideas collected in the blue folders and decide which ones are promising enough to be transferred to the pink folders and become a current discretionary project. If the unexpected time tidbit is short, he focuses on processing the fairly routine response type items in the manilla folders.

The key to using such tidbits of time is to control your anger at losing time and be physically prepared with working materials (it may also help to have a large briefcase and a strong arm!). Clark Kerr, the renowned labor relations scholar and president of the University of California, was once asked how he managed to publish so many papers while heading the nation's largest university. He replied that he did all of his writing in airport waiting rooms. Like the proverbial boy scout, he was always prepared.

Single Handling

Alec Mackenzie is particularly critical of multiple handling of memos, letters, and reports,[12] as in the following scenario. A letter arrives at a manager's desk; she scans it and allocates it to a particular category based on priority and topic; the piece of paper is placed in the appropriate "pending" box; later, the manager pulls it out from the pile and rereads the material before dictating a rough draft reply; when typed, the rough draft is checked and revisions written on it; finally, the finished draft is read and signed. In this method a single piece of paper is handled four times. It is Mackenzie's contention that most of this is unnecessary, wasteful, and actually an excuse for procrastination.

If you want to increase the number of items you handle only once, multiple consideration can be reduced. Of course you cannot and should not make immediate decisions on all issues. Discipline is required. It is also a matter of attitude. The attitude, however, is facilitated by certain techniques.

Writing on the original. Many letters can be answered by simply writing directly on the original. Return the original with your comments and keep a photocopy. Typing all interorganizational correspondence on printed company letterhead may be an expensive vanity. If your handwriting is illegible, keep a typewriter beside your desk and use it for short notes stapled to the original.

Prepared forms.   Forms are useful for responding to routine inquiries. From a quick survey of inquiries most frequently received, a general form listing standard alternative replies can often be prepared with very little trouble. Then, when an inquiry is received, the appropriate reply can simply be checked, and the form can be dispatched in very few minutes.

Minimizing dictation.   The central time-wasting problem with dictation is using it to postpone final decisions. A manager dictates a tentative reply onto a tape knowing that it will be some time before he receives the typed version from his secretary or the word processing group. He knows that he will be able to veto or revise his earlier position, perhaps even dictate an entirely new report.

But this can go on and on. The advantage of typing a rough draft yourself is that it seems more "real" than words on a tape. The manager can see immediately what it will look like in final draft. Perhaps he can simply order it typed and authorize the secretary to sign his name. Thus multiple handling is reduced.

Of course there is risk in such single-handling techniques. Mistakes that might have been caught by multiple readings may slip through. In addition, Peter Drucker warns us, such decisiveness is not always a virtue. Gypsy Rose Lee once observed, "Anything that is worth doing well is worth doing slowly." Drucker agrees, particularly with respect to personnel problems, which he feels should be handled slowly.[13] Decisions regarding hiring, firing, promoting, transferring, and evaluating should be made only after enough data have been gathered. Such personnel decisions should be made slowly, Drucker maintains, because they have long-lasting effects and are predominantly one-way. It is much easier to hire than to fire, to promote than to demote, and to assign than to relieve.

That slowness of decision is desirable was sharply brought to my attention when I first started my work in the United States Senate. Then minority leader Howard Baker of Tennessee said he hoped I was not an "efficiency expert" trying to make the Senate more efficient. He argued that the Senate is not supposed to be efficient, that bills should travel slowly to provide time for close examination, to correct weaknesses, and to have democracy work its will (one could argue, however, that three years to write an energy bill is a trifle long!).

Handling your briefcase. Mackenzie's major point on single handling, however, is that most matters can and should be decided on a single pass across the manager's desk. Unfortunately, the briefcase can be used to procrastinate. Putting

items into your briefcase to deal with later at home during insulated prime time is a legitimate tactic. The problem is that we are not always honest with ourselves or others. Sometimes what goes into the briefcase are those matters we dislike handling or are unable to make a decision on during the day. They may not really be important, just unpleasant.

Worse, the bulging briefcase can reflect a martyr complex. We want others and especially family to see how hard we are working. In a perverse way, taking work home convinces us that we are really important. Worst of all, the briefcase can be used to manipulate our families. If they exert demands on us to fix this broken appliance or play that juvenile game, we can point to the tyrannizing briefcase and complain that "I'd like to, but I can't." We may not even be aware of the deceit we thus practice on ourselves and others. Miraculously, the insistent demands of the briefcase papers can evaporate when there is a movie or game we would like to see!

CHAPTER 6

Fighting Procrastination

For all too many of us all too frequently, the most difficult time management task is overcoming procrastination. Let's consider its causes and possible treatments.

Causes of Procrastination

When you were a child did you eat your spinach first or last? It could have been cauliflower or broccoli but almost all of us had some vegetable we just hated to eat; however, our parents simply enforced a rule of no dessert until *all* of the main course was eaten, including the loathsome vegetable.

Assuming you really want that sweet reward at dinner's end, your two polar choices are to eat the spinach first and then be home free or save it until last just before the ice cream. No data exists on what percentage opts for either course, but the dilemma is suggestive of how personality affects time management. Effective time managers seem to consume the spinach of their jobs first.

Procrastinators in contrast seem to put off the spinach in hope that the demanding parent will relax his or her guard and forget to enforce the rule. More often than not, such delays don't work. Procrastination stems from complex causes that may well require a Freudian's couch to unravel. We can't do that here, but we can describe some behavioral habits of procrastinators.

I might fail.   Perfectionists frequently procrastinate. Such people passionately want to do things exactly right and experience great tension when confronted with a task that is "impossible." More precisely, it is very difficult to begin a task that has no universally accepted criteria for excellence.

The "Seabees" of World War II fame had a motto, "The difficult we do right now; the impossible will take a little longer." What the Seabees celebrated was their ability not to produce perfection but something that would do the job.

Most managerial problems don't lend themselves to perfect answers. Thus managers need to be able to tolerate some uncertainty about how well the task has been performed. Such tolerance usually means living with the anxiety that the procrastinating perfectionist strives to avoid. And "strive" is the correct word because some of us *work* to avoid starting projects that we dimly feel can't be done perfectly.

My self-image might be tarnished. Some very bright young people suffer from another self-delusion: that they are so good that they really don't have to do anything to prove it. This is actually a variant of the "I might fail" excuse, but is even more dishonest. These procrastinators are developing an advanced alibi. They never fail because they never try. Their illusion of mastery is never challenged because they never fail. They can go on deceiving themselves that they could have performed the great feat if they had "wanted to."

Unfortunately for their reputations, such procrastinators rapidly lose credibility in others' eyes. Their behavior is judged as particularly immature.

The time is not right. People who don't really believe they can control their lives look for external events to get them going.[1] They want clear cues of unknown origins to tell them when they should begin a difficult task. They may even turn to astrology, numerology, biorhythm, or some other method of prognostication in their search for encouragement or discouragement. Such a person may well delay starting a diet until an appropriate time, such as a "Monday" or the "first of the month" or even a first of a month that is a Monday. Control over one's life is abdicated in favor of chance.

Achievement-oriented, managerial-type people are not likely to deceive themselves by this form of procrastination.

I'll reward myself first. Earlier I distinguished between two types of people based on whether as children they ate a disliked vegetable such as spinach first or last. But the point is not so humorous with respect to procrastination. We human beings suffer from an unbelievable ability to deceive ourselves. When faced with an unpleasant task we may wrestle with the fundamental decision of whether or not to do it at all. After agonizing deliberation, we have courageously convinced ourselves to proceed. Self-applause for the hero!

Unfortunately, we may be so pleased with our apparent intention to begin that we tell ourselves that the chore is as good as done. Why not reward ourselves now? So some of us do. The student reasons, "I've decided to write the paper this weekend, so I deserve to go to the movies tonight." Or the manager thinks, "I'm going to crack down on the lax discipline around here next week, so this week I'll do what I like to do."

Delay may not always be bad, of course, and self-rewards are entirely appropriate—as long as they follow not precede substantive progress on the undesirable task. Rewarding yourself before you even begin often destroys the motivation to begin. Once you've dispensed the reward to yourself, what's the point of accomplishing the task? Or so some procrastinators ask.

Alas, no magic potion to cure procrastination or modern vaccine to prevent the illness is available. The disease is universal but it is not necessarily terminal.

Tactics for Overcoming Procrastination

Certain techniques can be helpful in dealing with procrastination. Five of the most useful tactics are setting deadlines for beginning, generating momentum, rewarding yourself for progress, including others in rewards, and discounting in advance.

Set deadlines for beginning. This can appear to be an excuse for delaying rather than starting immediately. But not every task can be started now so deadlines are appropriate. Of course, not only must you lead yourself to water but you must also force yourself to begin.

Generate momentum. Some people have trouble starting a task in the morning or after lunch. A tough, ambiguous, deferrable, procrastinable task can be extremely discouraging. Momentum can be developed, however, by beginning with some easy, programmed tasks such as routine correspondence and bureacratic detail. But set a time limit on how long you will do this and stick to it. A desk alarm set for thirty minutes will signal you to stop the easy and start the difficult. Don't be sucked in by the sense of achievement you may feel after completing the routine tasks. Give them up after a half hour. Confront the ambiguous.

Reward yourself for progress. All big, complex projects have smaller parts that you can celebrate as they are accomplished. Small self-rewards like a coffee break or even an afternoon off to play golf are justified if they mark significant progress on a lengthy project. Just be scrupulously honest with yourself that they follow and not precede or replace the actual work.

Include others in rewards. One of the sad aspects of modern work life is that it is divorced from family life. Children and spouse may not even know when wife or husband, Mom or Dad has accomplished something significant on the job. Perhaps you could invite them to a small dinner time ritual. Have a little ceremony; tell of your progress and of your ultimate goal. Give yourself a small gift that can be shared with other family members. And thank them for their implicit support of your work. After a while, they may begin to share more with you and the exchange of small rewards will become mutual.

Discount in advance. No one is perfectly honest with him- or herself. Even the healthiest of us use certain games or neuroticisms to deal with difficulty. Discounting is one of the most useful devices (and basically "healthy" if not done to excess).

Discounting means imaginatively projecting yourself into the future after the completion of the task and in advance dealing with inevitable disappointment. When the job is actually completed you will have already worked through the fact that the result is not exactly as you wished.

A certain fatalism characterizes this technique, of course, but it is not crippling if you feel that for the most part the results reflect not chance but your effort. It is just a recognition that you are not omnipotent and that perfection is impossible.

Some people term such discounting in advance as "settling for less." Perhaps it is, but I feel there is a slight distinction and the difference is important to me. Settling for less implies lowering your aspirations or relaxing your standards. This might be necessary, but it can be corrupting. In contrast, discounting implies maintaining aspirations and standards, striving to reach them, but maturely recognizing their probable impossibility.

The moral of the spinach tale is that effective time management usually includes the courage to confront the difficult and unpleasant early, sooner rather than later. When the spinach-first people were in high school, they probably started Saturday's chores on Friday afternoon, so that if something interesting turned up in the morning they would be free. In college they probably tried to get at least a solid hour of afternoon study in before dinner (worth two hours of late night time).

These examples suggest that effective time managers approach job and life much like their watches: they are always a little ahead. That is, they seldom accept other people's deadlines, *but create artificial earlier deadlines.*

Although this would seem to increase the pressure on them, such self-set artificial deadlines seem to have the opposite effect. Such people create the illusion of being a little more in control of time. They know they have a little leeway beyond the artificial deadline, but they almost never use it.

A college roommate of mine was one of the best time managers I've ever met. He simply refused to engage in mad-typing-a-paper-all-night-before-the-morning-class-at-which-it-was-due. And he never studied a particular subject the night before the examination. He set his deadlines twenty-four hours in advance. He might occasionally pull "an all-nighter" if necessary, but he would do it a day ahead of time. When we were trying to cover everything at the last minute he had a serenity that helped him fit ideas together in creative ways whereas we could only regurgitate as fast as we could write.

In short, effective time managers try to manipulate time rather than let time manipulate them. No one is entirely successful at this, but the effort seems to create an illusion of self-control, which makes the battle easier.

The Necessity for Responsiveness

Consider the mental patient who suffers from what psychiatrists call "the God complex."[3] *His* time is more valuable than others', *his* time is correct, *he* alone is justified in being unpunctual, and *his* prediction of future events alone will be fulfilled. Although not so disastrously, this distortion can afflict hard-charging, egocentric executives. In striving to improve their management of time, they must avoid becoming too self-centered in assuming that allocation of their time is the critical variable in the organization. Just as with some management literature, they may assume the following progression.

better manage-ment of personal time	$\Longrightarrow$	improved personal effectiveness	$\Longrightarrow$	improved organizational performance

In fact, they may be manipulating themselves and others to suit their own desires. The progression might actually be as follows.

better manage- ment of personal time	$\Longrightarrow$	more satisfying personal behavior	$\Longrightarrow$	deteriorated organizational performance

For example, one survey of 179 executives states: "The telephone does even more [than meetings] to prevent these top-level executives from making the most effective use of their time . . . 87 percent of the executives spend an hour or more on the telephone each day, and 40 percent spend a minimum of two hours."[4] What nonsense! The survey does not explain why talking on the phone is wasting time. Are no important deals arranged on the phone? Is not critical information tracked down? Are no sincere expressions of gratitude conveyed to a distant associate? Of course they are, and this is not wasted time.

Another article maintains that many executives agree they waste time listening.[5] "I get up in the morning and the phone rings and things go downhill from there," complains one company president. Another president says that 70 percent of his time is spent just listening and half that time is wasted "on things you'd avoid if you had any way of appraising them in advance." To imply that time is wasted *just because it is used in an unplanned way* is a distortion of values, a misguided overconcern for time at the expense of the job. Behind this distortion lies the unspoken assumption that unless a manager controls his own behavior and does only what he intends to do, he is wasting time. Even in profit-seeking business, this is an exaggeration bordering on absurdity.

When responding, managers must consider several problems simultaneously (or very closely sequenced) whereas in their own initiatives they concentrate on one issue at a time. This is a central difference between response time and discretionary time. The former is diffuse and problems are simultaneous; the latter is focused and problems are sequential. Short of isolation from others, it is simply impossible for managers always to do first things first and one at a time.

However attractive autonomy and discretionary control is, a warning is necessary:

1. No manager can or should manage all his time.
2. Response time is not necessarily wasted; it can be very effective in contributing to the organization.
3. Managers should be wary of managing their time in their own personal interest rather than the organization's.

Avoiding a stacked desk.   Another way of dividing people is into horizontal and vertical strata. As a horizontal person, I like to be surrounded at work by flat areas—large desk, table, shelves. In this horizontal area are stacked various piles of folders, papers, and memos. Each pile represents one of Mackenzie's major responsibility categories or Drucker's discretionary projects. As I gaze over these various piles I can form a mental picture of what I have to do. The piles are visual reminders.

Unfortunately, these piles on a stacked desk can also waste time. Alec Mackenzie is particularly critical of them

From the *Wall Street Journal*, reprinted by permission of Cartoon Features Syndicate.

because they can interfere with concentration and communication.[6] You can conceive of each stack as a little radio
transmitter sending out messages that trigger the receiver
in your brain. And they can be sending simultaneously! As
you look up from the work immediately before you on your
desk, your attention can be distracted by the waves from
each pile. And each pile represents dreams, problems, and
anxieties that nag at you as you try to return to your immediate work. These mini-transitions undermine your efficiency and waste time.

And it is even worse when someone is trying to talk to
you across the piles. Your attention may wander as your
eyes alight on a pile, or your pending volume of work can
inadvertently cause you to communicate your anxiety to
your visitor. Your very body language of shuffling papers,
playing with a pencil, or repeatedly glancing at your watch
will make your caller feel uncomfortable.

One of the most satisfying moments in my research in
the United States Senate came when a senior senator invited
me to talk in his hideaway Capitol office. It was a delightful
small colonial room with high ceilings. The walls were covered with a multitude of framed photographs of the past.
Pictures of the senator with presidents, constituents, and
family were displayed alongside antiques of his politically
active father and grandfather. The problem was that each of
the pictures carried emotional baggage. As I talked, the senator's eyes moved around the room, and I could sense his
attention fading in and out. Perhaps this partially reflected
the strength of my message, but I think it also reflected the
interference from the pictures.

Such inattention may discourage people from initiating
talks. Worse, you may actually be glad to be left alone to
concentrate on your work. But the cost can be heavy because
you may be cut off from essential information. You will learn
only what you ask about specifically. Little that is sponta-
neous will come your way if your visitors feel they are only
interrupting.

Better to be a vertical person according to Mackenzie.

Such a person keeps his folders filed in a vertical cabinet until needed. The only material on his or her desk is what is being worked on at the moment. If you are unable to limit yourself to such files and you simply must have horizontal space, better to have it behind your desk so you and your visitors don't have to peer through or over your piles of papers. Better yet if the piles can be hidden by a curtain.

This may seem like trivial detail, but the point is an important one. Concentration is likely to be stronger and communication more effective if you and your office convey an atmosphere of serenity and no time pressures are evident.

Being available. An important problem for executives is keeping themselves informed. Studies suggest that they do not participate in many decisions and seldom issue orders.[9] Since they are so dependent on information, executives initiate many inquiries and conversations. In spite of the importance of initiating communications, however, high-level executives depend even more upon others bringing information to them. They must be open and receptive to communications from subordinates and associates. That this is an effective style is suggested by my finding that *executives rated more highly by their superiors spend more time than lower-rated executives advising and discussing with people who come to them.*[8] High-rated executives spend less time in communications that they initiate than in responding. The hours are indicated in Table 2. Apparently effective general executives develop their various relationships so that others feel free to come to them.

Shortly after the death of Winston Churchill, Sir Anthony Eden discussed what he considered Churchill's outstanding leadership characteristic. He said that the indefatigable former prime minister always seemed to be available, he was ready to listen, he never cut off a suggestion with a curt dismissal but encouraged elaboration. To be sure, the great man was often formidable and abusive to subordinates who made mistakes in policy implementation. And he could be dictatorial in ordering the conduct of his

Table 2.   Number of Hours per Week Spent in Communication Activities by "Less Effective" and "More Effective" General Executives ($N = 14$)*

Activity	"Less Effective" Executives	"More Effective" Executives
	hours	*hours*
Responding: advising, discussing	9.5	16.0
Initiating: consulting, discussing	11.3	6.5

* Differences are statistically significant at .05 level.

own policy. Nonetheless he was invariably receptive to new ideas. It was not a threatening experience to broach a new matter with Churchill. Consequently, he was approached— and some of the unsolicited ideas were good.

It appears that similar behavior characterizes effective business executives. Anthony Jay terms this approachability "keeping his feedback nerves as raw and sensitive as possible."

> This also involves listening to criticism from his subordinates. . . . Churchill was alive to feedback and Goering was not. The successful creative leader is often willing to listen to criticism from anybody from his vice-president to the office cleaner, and his subordinates are often infuriated when they discover the lowly source of the complaints which are being forwarded to them.[9]

Mentally separating response time and discretionary time helps to maintain responsiveness to others. A manager should decide that certain periods are to be primarily response time. She may work on discretionary matters if no one contacts her, but she should not expect to accomplish anything discretionary. If she does, it is an unexpected bonus. This orientation toward response will help her to overcome the natural irritation of having outside events interfere with self-determined plans. Thus self-discipline is essential to create a climate of openness and responsiveness.

Managers should strive to project an unrushed image, to avoid appearing preoccupied with their own concerns, and to give subordinates their undivided attention. No one expects perfect attention every time, but some is imperative. A manager needs to show that he values the other person's proposal. A subordinate's respect for himself and for his superior would be undermined without it. Such behavior takes more time in the short run, but because of more effective relations programs may be achieved that no amount of time would otherwise make possible.

Research also suggests that *effective executives conduct more of their discussions in intimate two-person talks than in group meetings or via correspondence.*[10] Effective executives extend invitations to individuals to come see them personally rather than wait for the next scheduled meeting. Obviously, this is an untidy way to operate. It consumes much precious time. Yet executives derive benefits from a two-person style: it facilitates the frank expression of opinions and ideas without antagonizing others that would be present in a group meeting.

Availability and openness to subordinates and associates are imperative for managers if they do not want to lose touch with their organizations. They cannot possibly initiate enough interrogations to maintain control. Being available is a necessity because timing is so important. If the executive is not available when needed to supply information or support, his subordinates may lose interest and drive.

By controlling all their time, reducing response time, and lessening others' autonomy, some managers may centralize the organization in order to reduce ambiguity and threat at the cost of future performance. They could be guilty of the hazard of efficiency—efficiency that wastes the time of others.

CHAPTER 7

Tying Time to Objectives

"Now that I've retired, I have time for all the things I dreamed of doing, but I forget what they were!"

From the *Wall Street Journal*, reprinted by permission of Cartoon Features Syndicate.

Effectiveness is more important than efficiency. In time management, means and ends can get confused. The various time diaries, logs, and inventories become an end in themselves if keeping track of time becomes more important than what is done with it. The purpose of all the tactics is not to save time itself, but to allow time for accomplishing important tasks. My own preference in time management is to focus on organizational objectives and how work time is allocated to accomplish them. Therefore we first must discuss management planning and then show how personal time relates to organizational objectives and goals.

Perspectives on Planning

The definitions of planning are numerous: thinking about what you want and how you are going to accomplish it; determining in advance what is to be done; preparing for the future by making decisions now.[1] Planning represents management's attempt to anticipate the future and guard itself against the threat of change, which humans are urgently aware of because of their time sense. Planning is our effort to visualize "the future as history" by determining how we would want the future to appear if we could jump ahead in time and look backward.[2] "The purpose of planning," according to one executive, "is not to show how precisely we can predict the future, but rather to uncover the things we must do today in order to have a future."

Beautiful thoughts, but tough to act upon! All managers have to face the nagging reality of their jobs—pressure to concentrate on the present, ignore the past, and let tomorrow take care of itself. Managers who are so taken in, however, are not exercising human leadership to its fullest potential. Behaviorally and psychologically, management should be oriented toward the future, carving time out of the present in the service of tomorrow. "The ideal executive," maintains one corporation chairman, "should have a feel for the future, not only from the standpoint of where his or her own business is going, but where competitors are going, what other industries are doing, and what is happening to the country."

Continuing objectives for business. A firm's strategy comes to life through the formulation of management's continuing objectives.[3] These are the long-run, ongoing concerns for at least the next five years and probably the next ten years.

In some ultimate sense, the central business objective is profit, but a firm will not survive unless it pays attention to some additional objectives. Here is Peter Drucker's list of multiple objectives:[4]

- Profitability: gross profit or net profits as a percentage of funds invested in the business
- Market standing: the proportion of the market enjoyed compared with competitors
- Productivity: relation of output of goods or services to input of resources such as labor, materials, and money
- State of resources: protection and maintenance of equipment, buildings, inventory, and funds
- Service: timely and appropriate quality response to customers' and clients' needs
- Innovation: development and delivery of new products or services
- Social contribution/public responsibility: improvement of environment and quality of life

Process objectives for all organizations. The business objectives described above emphasize results, but we also need to recognize process objectives that apply to business and all other institutions. Behavioral scientist Warren Bennis argues that time must be allocated to the process objectives or an organization will not be successful for very long.[5] His process objectives include the following:

- Identification: achieving clarity, consensus, and commitment to organizational objectives
- Integration: integrating individual needs and organizational objectives.
- Social influence: distributing power and authority effectively
- Collaboration: producing mechanisms for the control of conflict among staff members

- Adaptation: responding appropriately to changes induced by the organization's environment
- Revitalization: dealing with internal growth and decay

Note that these continuing objectives have no priorities, numbers, or time limits. They simply define in qualitative terms the values that characterize the organization. Most companies do not have a written statement embracing all their continuing objectives. Rather these objectives exist in the combined minds of various executives and come into play only when specific goals are being formulated.

The following is a statement of continuing objectives published by Johnson & Johnson under the headline "Our Credo":

We believe our first responsibility is to the doctors, nurses and patients, to mothers and all others who use our products and services. In meeting their needs everything we do must be of high quality. We must constantly strive to reduce our costs in order to maintain reasonable prices. Customers' orders must be serviced promptly and accurately. Our suppliers and distributors must have an opportunity to make a fair profit.

We are responsible to our employees, the men and women who work with us throughout the world. Everyone must be considered as an individual. We must respect their dignity and recognize their merit. They must have a sense of security in their jobs. Compensation must be fair and adequate, and working conditions clean, orderly and safe. Employees must feel free to make suggestions and complaints. There must be equal opportunity for employment, development and advancement for those qualified. We must provide competent management, and their actions must be just and ethical.

We are responsible to the communities in which we live and work and to the world community as well. We must be good citizens—support good works and charities and bear our fair share of taxes. We must encourage civic improvements and better health and education. We must maintain in good order the property we are privileged to use, protecting the environment and natural resources.

Our final responsibility is to our stockholders. Business must make a sound profit. We must experiment with new ideas. Research must be carried on, innovative programs developed and mistakes paid for. New equipment must be purchased, new facilities provided and new products launched. Reserves must be created to provide for adverse times. When we operate according to these principles, the stockholders should realize a fair return.

Many people are skeptical about such written statements (especially when profits are mentioned last) and see them as merely public relations gimmicks designed to promote the firm. Although such cynicism is perhaps understandable, we cannot assume that the sole continuing business objective is profit.

Setting Specific Goals

In the above listings of objectives for both business and other organizations I did not deal with the contradiction between some of them but simply listed the various objectives without considering how they operate together. Simultaneously expanding profits and market share, for example, may be impossible because price cuts may be necessary to get new customers. And improving productivity and curbing pollution may be mutually exclusive because pollution control equipment tends to increase operating costs. When management sets goals to be accomplished in a specific time period —next week, month, year, or decade—it has to deal with conflict among the continuing objectives.[6]

Setting priorities. The beginning of the conversion from non-specific objectives to specific goals is setting priorities. A firm's multiple objectives can be arrayed along a continuum of most dominant to most deferrable. Most dominant are those that demand everyday attention. Deferrable objectives are those that can safely be ignored for short periods of time. The executive team of a private power company defined their objectives as shown in Figure 4.

Clearly the central purpose of this company is to design and construct electrical equipment so that customers will have sufficient energy when it is needed. And the company

**Figure 4. Objectives Determined for an Engineering and Re-
search Division of an Investor-owned Public Utility Company**

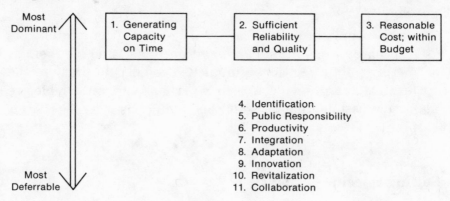

must do this with the financial resources available. These
are the dominant objectives.

Note, however, how high in importance the executive
team ranked identification. They put it immediately after
their top three objectives. One might think that a stable
business such as a power company would have long since
settled its identification issue. Yet, the activities of this firm
showed several glaring contradictions. On the first floor of
their building was a retail store operated by the marketing
department that sold electricity-consuming appliances such
as ranges, refrigerators, air conditioners, and heating units.
On the top floor, however, top management was worrying
about how it could possibly meet the region's energy needs
next summer if the temperature reached ninety-five degrees!
Marketing was trying to increase energy consumption while
top executives were trying to deal with the need for conser-
vation.

Public responsibility—ranked fifth—was of increasing
concern because of criticism from an apparently ever expanding array of groups. Top management had to incorpo-
rate into any engineering design increasing public demands,
such as those for more appealing transmission towers (or
underground cables) and for prevention of river thermal pollution.

Objectives like adaptation and revitalization—ranked eighth and tenth, respectively—were deemed deferrable. The consensus of the executive team was that these objectives could safely be postponed without immediate adverse impact on the firm's performance. Only a voice or two in the group asked whether the company had already delayed too long on these matters, whether in the past too little time had been allocated to these nonspecific objectives so that disaster now loomed near.

Consider one incident. The company lagged in using computers in its engineering design. Of course a computer handled payroll, billing, and cost accounting, but the design professionals still used desk calculators. No on-line interaction was provided with the computer. In contrast, designers in advanced electronics firms have computer terminals on their desks. They can call out already designed components from the stored memory, move them around the CRT screen with a "magic pen" into a desired configuration, push a button, and produce a hard drawing.

To advance the design process, a department manager in the power company decided to hire a scientific computer systems expert. He discovered, however, that to hire an experienced person he would have to pay over $40,000 per year—which was substantially more than he made! And even if he was willing to pay a subordinate more than his own salary, the firm's personnel policies would not have allowed it. Therefore, the manager hired a less experienced man for $23,000 per year. The young man failed, however, because he didn't have the experience or personal clout necessary (and besides he had long hair down to his shoulders in an organization where most of the engineers had crew cuts).

That was a revitalization issue. The firm's policy arteries were so inflexible that it couldn't adapt to labor market realities. Its internal world was out of touch with its environment. The engineering department's managers' low placement of revitalization on the most-dominant—most-deferrable continuum is both cause and effect of not carving time out of the present to deal with such long-range matters.

To convert objectives into accomplishment (especially the more deferrable objectives), they must be transformed into specific goals.

A goal for every objective.   For each continuing objective there should be one or more specific goals for the next relevant time period and a specific indicator by which performance is to be measured. Some examples for a manufacturing company are given in Table 3.

Less measurable goals.   If a continuing objective has no parallel specific goal for the next appropriate time period, managers are unlikely to devote much attention to it. Their energies will be focused on the specific goals by which their

Table 3.   Some Objectives and Goals for a Manufacturing Company

Continuing Objective	Specific Goal for Coming Year	Performance Indicator
Provide a fair return on investment	Provide a 15 percent rate of return; up 5 percent from last year	Net profits for year as a percentage of net invested capital ($125 million)
Ensure an important share of the market	Retain 75 percent of old customers	Percentage of people whose last purchase was from us who replace item with new purchase from us
	Capture 25 percent of first-time purchasers	Percentage of people purchasing item for first time who purchase from us
Manufacture goods efficiently	Improve productivity by 5 percent	No. parts produced per week divided by the total hours of labor utilized per week. Installation of new punching machine by August 1

performance is being evaluated.[7] Simply stating that "high employee morale" is a continuing objective is unlikely to influence managers concerned about the net rate of return on investment, market share, and productivity. Even stating that the manager's goal is to "improve morale by 15 percent" in the next year will have little impact if no indicator is defined or no measurement is taken. To motivate the manager to attempt to improve morale would require more specificity, such as, for example, "reduce turnover by 15 percent" or improve the score on Professor Jones's attitude survey by 15 percent."

It would be great if the performance indicator in fact measured the specific goal and its contribution to the relevant continuing objective. On the more easily quantifiable objectives, such as profitability and productivity, this is clear. With objectives such as morale, however, the relationship between indicators and continuing objectives is more uncertain. We are not sure that turnover or Jones's questionnaire really measure morale, but at least they make an effort to do so. Otherwise, no attention will be paid to morale.

Unfortunately, not all of the continuing objectives can be converted into numerical specific goals. How does one quantify public responsibility? Being a good citizen? Achieveman of identification, collaboration, or revitalization? Because such objectives are difficult to measure with numbers, management must often settle for words that suggest what behavior would probably help in reaching the desired objectives. For example, contributing to the United Fund and to private colleges may add to meeting social responsibility, not breaking laws is part of good citizenship, conflict can be managed better if strikes are few, or hiring new managers may produce revitalization. These are plausible conclusions, but proving them with numbers is impossible.[8] Table 4 gives some statements of relevant behavior that serve as performance indicators for less measurable objectives in a manufacturing company.

Table 4.   Some More Difficult to Measure Objectives and Goals for a Manufacturing Company

Continuing Objective	Specific Goal for Coming Year	Performance Indicator
Develop middle management for executive responsibilities	Develop a merit review system for middle managers	Report submitted to V.P. by December 1
	Send ten managers to university executive programs	Number of managers sent by January 1
Be a good corporate citizen	Reduce air pollution at plant by 15 percent	By January 1 pollution output should be 125 lbs./hr. (or less) measured at stack by electrostatic test
Provide a safe and satisfying workplace for employees	Eliminate dangerous conditions in Plant B by automating the loading operation	Installation of the new loader should be 50 percent complete by end of year. Deadline is in 18 months.
	Reduce injuries by 10 percent	Employee-days lost to injuries/Total employee-days available for year

From Organization Plans to Personal Time Management

This lengthy discussion of planning is necessary to show how one's individual time management can be tied into the organization's plans. Figure 5 illustrates the form for an individual manager's "Master Weekly Time Plan." The left-hand column should contain the continuing objectives of the manager's unit, arrayed in order of most dominant to most deferrable. The term "unit" refers to the logical organizational entity to which the manager belongs. Thus, in Figure 6, X could be the president of the firm or the head of a major division, A, the head of a division or department within the firm, and B, department head or supervisor.

Figure 5.   Format for a Master Weekly Time Plan

1. Unit's Continuing Objectives	2. Subunit's Specific Goals	3. Subunit's Performance Indicators	To Be Done		
			Immediate (this week)	Short Run (this month)	Long Run (this year)
A.					
B.					
C.					
D.					
E.					
F.					

Most Dominant ↑

Most Deferrable ↓

Figure 6.   Organization Units and Subunits

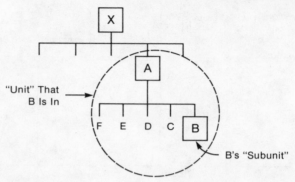

Master weekly time plan.   Let us focus on manager B's individual master time plan. The first column will be the continuing objectives for the whole unit headed by manager A. These objectives could be developed in one of two ways.

- The best option would be a management-by-objectives type meeting (or meetings) whereby manager A and subordinates B through F (in Figure 6) reach consensus on the unit's continuing objectives and their arrangement along the continuum.[9]
- Almost equally useful for B's time management would be good authoritarian leadership by A who defines the unit's continuing objectives and announces them to his subordinates.

In either of these two approaches the unit's objectives would have to be defined in a manner consistent with X's strategy and objectives for the whole organization, of course.

Since the continuing objectives pertain to the unit, the first column is identical on the personal time plans for managers B, C, D, E, and F. Columns 2 and 3 are likely to be unique for each manager, however, because they apply only to his subunit. The entries on B's second and third column can also be developed in either of two ways.

- Again preferred is a management-by-objectives approach where A and B negotiate an agreement of what specific goals B and his subunit will pursue in the next relevant time period (most likely a year) to contribute to the unit's continuing objectives.

- Also workable is good top-down planning where A informs B of the subunit's specific goals and the criteria by which performance will be judged.

After the unit's objectives and B's subunit goals and performance indicators have been defined, they will be reproduced on B's full-year supply of master time plans. Thus he will be repeatedly reminded of what he is trying to accomplish as he plans for each week.

Scheduling time. The form's right-hand side is blank and can be used to schedule activities and reserve blocks of discretionary time. The titles of the three right-hand columns could be varied to suit the individual user's needs. I envision the following use, however: "immediate" refers to activities that must be performed this week; "short run" means this month, and "long run" this year.

By and large the most dominant activities will get done; these are the items that get onto the "to be done" lists of even the poorest time managers. The individual master time plan, however, forces you to confront the longer-run and more deferrable projects. Every week and every day you are reminded of your obligation to the future through the more deferrable objectives and goals. In scanning a past year's set of weekly time plans, you should see that daily entries move from the "long-run" column to the "short-run" column to the "immediate" column.

Thus, if attention is to be paid to the longer-run objectives and goals, immediate time must be allocated to them. The main purpose of the individual master time plan for the week is to remind you of your managerial purposes and to force you to confront the need to convert the long run into the short run and the immediate.

Daily time plan. Many effective time managers develop unique forms for their daily schedules and "to do" lists. Figure 7 presents a useful format. It is divided into two main sections: (A) today's activities and (B) today's communications. The two sides of the form are not mutually exclusive,

Figure 7.   Format for a Daily Time Plan

A. Today's Activities	B. Today's Communications
1. Most Dominant, must be done today	1. Scheduled Meetings
	Time Name(s)
2. More Deferrable, discretionary	2. Other People to See/Telephone
3. Personal	3. People to Write to

of course, because performing the activities will require communicating with people. But, as suggested in Chapter 3, dominant activities should not totally determine whom you communicate with during any single day. The time plan's right side will assist you in tending to relationships as a separate agenda.

Your time plan for each day should be made the evening before or as your first task each morning. Additional entries can be made as the day progresses. Most dominant activities are those that you must complete that day. More deferrable activities are discretionary tasks that you would like to perform that day. Drawing on your master weekly time plan, you should strive to reserve blocks of time for discretionary activities as necessary. If possible, these blocks should be during your personal prime times.

Space is included for personal activities. As we shall see in Chapter 11, devoting adequate time to personal goals is important for maintaining a sense of control over one's time and life. And such self-mastery can contribute to your sense of confidence in dealing with job demands.

PART TWO
MANAGING LONGER-TERM TIME

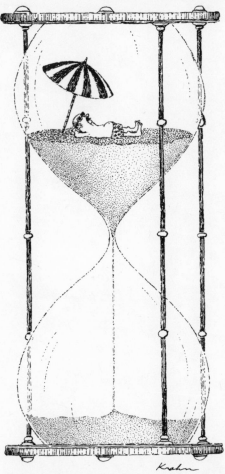

Drawing by Krahn; © 1963 The New Yorker
Magazine, Inc. Reprinted by permission.

CHAPTER 8

How the Past Enslaves

© King Features Syndicate, Inc., 1979. World rights reserved. Reprinted by permission.

"All history is bunk," Henry Ford I is reputed to have said.[1] What Mr. Ford was suggesting is that managers are concerned with the future, not the past. Their thoughts should be about future conditions, future events, and future returns. Accounting and finance teach us that past costs are gone; they should play no role in decisions about the future. In evaluating human performance, the control system should not emphasize punishment for past deeds but should be oriented toward improved performance in the future. Blindly adhering to past behavior is a major cause of wasted time.

Ironically, the Ford Motor Company dramatically illustrated that management loses when it persists in an obsolete strategy.[2] In his memoirs, Alfred Sloan, long-time chief executive at General Motors, points out that during the 1920s Ford did not recognize the historical development of public taste and the desire for increased choice and luxury.[3] Sloan understood, and General Motors responded in their product policy. Ford did not, and sales of the Model T declined more precipitously than had horse-drawn buggies a generation before. In 1927 almost no Model T's were sold. Ford had nothing else to offer until a year later when the Model A was unveiled—a car that Sloan thought to be old-fashioned even at its introduction.

Clinging to the Past

Blind obedience to the past is characteristic of certain neurotic individuals and their organizational counterparts. Psychiatrists tell us that a sense of identity is necessary in order to escape the pull of the past.[4] People with a compulsive neurosis demonstrate continued obedience to old conditioning demands; they rigidly obey mechanical orders in their historical sequences. They stick to tyrannical inner schedules out of fear of real life. Slavish adherence to the past, to the "old ways that are best" is a means of warding off the unknown with its associated anxiety. One can observe in some children the compulsion to repeat pleasure *ad nauseum* and unto utter exhaustion. Most of us occasionally cling anxiously to the past.

Persistence of inappropriate behavior.   Consider the following tale about the British army.[5] After France fell to the invading German army in 1940, Great Britain felt its own invasion was imminent. Guns were in short supply and the British pressed into service some venerable formerly horse-drawn artillery pieces left over from the turn-of-the-century Boer War. Hitched to light trucks, the guns would be hauled up and down the channel coast and various test firings were held at night. The English hoped to mislead Nazi intelligence into concluding that they had more artillery than they actually did.

Unfortunately, the gun was extremely slow in firing. A time study expert was brought in to determine how the firing rate could be improved. The engineer observed a five-man crew in action and took some slow-motion pictures. Studying the actions of the young soldiers, he noticed something odd: a moment before firing, two members ceased all movement and came to attention for a three-second interval extending through the firing of the weapon. He consulted an elderly colonel of artillery who was also puzzled but finally exclaimed, "I have it! They are holding the horses." The horses, of course, had long since gone the way of the Boer War and the youthful soldiers had not even been born when horses pulled the guns. But the old procedures were still being followed without thought even though they were incongruous in the present.

To the business manager this story may epitomize the limitations of the military mind. But all minds are quite similar in this regard. Consider my experience when working as a staff adviser at Eastman Kodak, certainly one of the world's best-managed firms.

Since silver is the most expensive raw material in photographic film, it pays to reprocess old and scrap film to recover the silver. Outdated film, production waste, and worn motion picture reels are sorted, chopped, and chemically treated to recover the silver and reuse the flexible base. One group concentrated on old motion picture film sent in from studios and distributors.

Monthly, the department reported to corporate headquarters on the count and physical condition of the film. When asked why the report was made, the department manager replied that it was required by headquarters. When asked if he used the data in the report in managing the department, he answered no. An inquiry at the corporate office resulted in my being shown the files of several years' reports. But the clerk indicated that no one ever looked at the files! What was going on?

Some historical digging revealed that the report originated back in the 1920s when motion picture film was on a nitrate base. Such material was and is extremely dangerous; it deteriorates with age and temperature and humidity changes to become spontaneously combustible and near explosive in the presence of a spark or flame. Thus the older and more dangerous reels were sorted first and a close tab was kept on the state of the film.

But by the 1960s when management was still making the report, nitrate base had long since been in disuse. In the mid-1930s Kodak had replaced the nitrate base with an acetate base which was much more stable and safer (the firm won a belated Academy Award for this in 1979). Yet the report on nitrate film was still being made twenty-five years after it was replaced and perhaps ten years after the last reel had passed through the department.

The danger in policies and procedures. Policies and procedures are essential to giving stability and control to organizations. Unfortunately, they also create problems because immediately after being written, they begin to become obsolete. Therefore, if they are followed blindly, management loses direction. Means and ends are inverted. To some people, rules become ends to be pursued without thought as to whether they actually contribute to the firm's objectives.

Such inversion of means and ends is almost synonymous with bureaucracy and organization. Business managers frequently assume that such distortion characterizes nonprofit institutions such as governments, schools, and hospitals. But business is not immune. An advertisement in a prominent management journal once showed a hand holding a notebook embossed in gold letters with the words *Policy Manual*. The notebook was suspended over a wire basket incinerator in which several notebooks were burning. Who was the advertiser? A management consulting firm. Their message? That one should not allow standing plans, policies, and procedures to exist unchanged for too long because they get out of date and hinder the organization instead of helping it. Better to burn them—and call in a consultant to compose a new set!

Joseph Hall, long-time chief executive at Kroger Company, suggested that his people should periodically change their view of their jobs. In order to forestall overreliance on the past, "I would tell them that they should, a couple of times a year, pretend they are a new man on the job. All right, one of the first things you do is just go through your desk and look at the files and clean them out; and everything that crosses your desk, you question: Why? Never take things for granted. I don't believe in tradition unless tradition is sound.[6]

Perhaps even more dangerous for the organization is that spontaneity disappears. Once established and accepted, policies and controls tend to limit flexibility and initiative. In the beginning at least, management gains in coordination and predictability what they may lose in initiative. Nonetheless, since policies, procedures, and controls are based on the past, it is difficult to keep them up to date: policies may no longer apply to new conditions, controls may measure irrelevant factors, and those rational plans which were developed to promote organizational effectiveness begin to interfere with the accomplishment of objectives. If managers blindly follow these rules, spontaneity is lost. Under long-standing restrictive control systems, some managers ignore whether mistakes are avoided or not. If they feel that punishment awaits any unsuccessful departure from procedure, managers may do what "the book" requires—and that's all. No spontaneity will be demonstrated and apathy will be prevalent.[7]

Resistance to Change

The most insidious attraction of the past can be that it worked. Because we are satisfied with what we are doing and because we perceive no threat, we repeat the past—perhaps until it is too late.

Consider another historical example, that of the introduction of continuous-aim naval gunfire in the United States Navy.[8] If you remember your late-night pirate movies on television, when two ships in the nineteenth century were to battle at sea, each would attempt to maneuver upwind of the other, shoot the other's marines out of the rigging, come alongside, throw a boarding ladder across and claim the other vessel as prize.

Such a sequence demonstrated the victor's superior seamanship. But actually the main reason for getting so close was that it was extremely difficult to hit the target at any range in any kind of sea. The problem was that until the end of the 1800s, even after ships were made of steel and began to look "modern," the guns were basically fixed in elevation with respect to the deck. As the ship rolled, the gun rolled. Thus the gun had to be fired, whether by fuse, mallet, or electrical spark, in anticipation of the roll, resulting in low accuracy.

In 1898 Sir Percy Scott, a British navy officer, introduced a change in the gearing mechanism on his guns that allowed a pointer to elevate and depress the barrel continuously thus keeping it on target as the ship rolled. Improved accuracy was astounding: on the order of 3000 percent.

The United States Navy knew nothing of this innovation until 1900 when a young lieutenant named William Sims observed some British test firings. He was much impressed and promptly reported his observations to his superiors. At first he received no reply; his letters were merely filed.

Sims, however, was persistent (and a little abrasive) and kept up the pressure by writing to the Bureau of Ordnance in Washington. The navy eventually ran a test at the Washington Naval Shipyard which, they contended, disproved Sims's report. The experimenters said they couldn't find anyone strong enough to continuously elevate and depress the gun.

Sims was extremely persistent and eventually directly contacted President Theodore Roosevelt. T.R. listened and appointed Sims as an inspector of naval ordnance. The change was soon introduced and Sims ended up an admiral in World War I.

But why was this clear-cut improvement initially rejected?

Rejection of change source. The Washington Navy Department gunnery officials did not see Sims as a legitimate source of change. After all, he was just a young line officer with no special expertise in ordnance. Besides he was literally half a world away.

The NIH ("not invented here") syndrome undoubtedly also played a role. Sims's initiative might have been threatening to the Washington experts. He was asking them to change the very guns they had designed. If the innovation was so good, their superiors might well have inquired why the headquarters' specialists didn't think of it.

Satisfaction with the present. A profound cause of resistance to change is that people may feel no need to change. They perceive no threat requiring them to change what has worked in the past.

The U.S. Navy in 1900 was still basking in the glow of their glorious victory at Manila Bay in the Spanish–American war. Admiral Dewey had led his flagship, the U.S.S. *Olympia,* and his fleet to defeat the supposed power of the Spanish monarchy (in fact, the Spanish ships were rusting to pieces). We were exulting in the new world power of the United States. The old gunnery system had triumphed. Why change?

When Sims finally achieved power in Washington, he checked all the reports on Manila Bay and determined that of 9,500 shots fired, only 121 had hit their targets! But this had been enough to win the battle. And it might have been good shooting for the old technology.

This bias toward the past may also have distorted the experiment conducted by ordnance officials. Rather than on the deck of a rolling vessel at sea, the test was conducted on concrete on land in a shipyard. Officials attempted to simulate the roll of the ship by having the pointer continuously elevate and depress the gun. But it required a lot of strength to move the gun whereas Sims had written that it was so easy at sea. He must be wrong, thought the experimenters.

But Sims was not wrong. Readers who remember their high school physics will recognize the problem. At sea Isaac Newton's first law of gravity is working for the pointer; on land it works against him. That is, a body at rest tends to stay at rest. On land the ordnance officials were attempting to move the gun continuously. At sea the pointer merely held the gun fixed *in space* while the ship rolled around it. The difference in force required was enormous.

Did the Washington experimenters intentionally sabotage the test? Probably not. More likely, their resistance to change prevented investing sufficient time and energy to prove the innovation's value.

Admission of your own ignorance.   The NIH syndrome springs from the difficulty of admitting that you didn't know there was a better way. Such admission can be extremely difficult if it means facing your own guilt in causing harm.

A classic illustration of such resistance comes from medicine. Ignaz Semmelweis was a Hungarian physician in charge of the maternity clinic at Vienna University Hospital in 1847.[9] At the time the death rate in childbirth was very high—over 12 percent at his hospital. He sharply reduced this rate to approximately 1 percent by 1848 by having physicians disinfect their hands in carbolic acid before examining patients. Prior to this, attending doctors had just lightly washed or wiped their hands on their aprons and moved directly from pathology examination (even autopsies) to women in labor.

The physicians didn't like the change because the acid irritated their skin, and Semmelweis was dismissed from his post in 1849. By the following year, however, he had begun to repeat his success at a maternity ward in Budapest—to under 1 percent mortality. He published his findings in 1861. But once again he was rejected by the leading medical authorities. In 1865 he committed suicide in an insane asylum and has largely been forgotten.

Joseph Lister is not forgotten, however. In 1867, only two years after Semmelweis died, this English physician published a paper on how he used carbolic acid to clean the site of compound bone fractures (where skin has been punctured). His innovation took the medical world by storm and became widely celebrated. (Eventually Lister had a mouthwash named after him. No such fame befell the name of Semmelweis.)

Almost twenty years later, in the 1880s, a Hungarian doctor wrote by then Lord Lister telling him how Semmelweis had anticipated the use of a disinfectant. To his credit, Lister acknowledged Semmelweis's prior innovation and used his own great authority to get it accepted as standard procedure in maternity hospitals—fully forty years after the Hungarian had demonstrated that it could reduce maternal morality by more than 90 percent.

Why was Lister's procedure so easily accepted by physicians whereas they fought Semmelweis's for so long? Perhaps because the former's was consistent with the doctors' self-image: that is, they treated the wound and healed the patient. They were the agents of healing. In Semmelweis's case, however, to adopt his procedure required tacit admission that they themselves had been the agent of infection and death. This required a change in self-image that was inadmissible (besides, in the early nineteenth century a physician derived status from the blood and pus on his apron; it showed he was busy and in demand).

For an equally disturbing business example, consider the nuclear accident at the Three Mile Island generating plant that so frightened the world in 1979. A combination of technological weakness and human error led to increased radiation and the risk of a meltdown that might have resulted in widespread contamination and death.

President Carter appointed a commission to investigate the incident. Shortly after beginning its work, the group toured the undamaged control room at the generating plant. The chairman of the commission was John Kemeny, a renowned mathematician and president of Dartmouth College. In an informal press interview he reported that he was shocked by the condition of the control room.[10] It was impressive to the layman with its glowing dials and flashing lights, but he immediately recognized that even though the plant was only a year old, the control system was outdated by perhaps a decade!

Kemeny said that he asked the engineering vice president of the utility why they were using such obsolete technology in a new plant. The company executive, according to Kemeny, explained that the control system lagged because the firm's employees could handle a system that was only slightly more complex than what they were used to in the coal and oil plants. That is more frightening than the slight radiation that escaped. The future could not be dealt with because of the past limitations of the people involved.

A more modest and less disturbing business example of this misperception of the future world is provided by the owner–manager of a small print shop. He achieved success by concentrating on letterpress printing for a wide variety of local and regional customers. When lower-cost, but lower-quality, offset printing came along, the owner felt little need to add the new technology and offered a variety of excuses: "I don't have room. I don't have time. It produces lousy copy. None of my customers would accept it."

This resistance to new technology went along with his view that the local government, hospital, schools, and churches, were backward. They were good customers, but the owner–manager believed them to be badly managed, inefficient, and not greatly concerned about costs, as they all were nonprofit institutions. But he was wrong. As the cost pressures on these institutions increased, quality became a lesser concern and offset quality improved with time, anyway. He lost an opportunity to grow because of his misperception of the future.

Preference for existing authority patterns. Changes in the system of authority and status especially provoke resistance. Another military story illustrates this.[11]

The *Wampanoag* was one of the most successful U.S. naval vessels. Commissioned in 1868, she was 355 feet long, displaced 4,200 tons, and was heavily armed. Primary propulsion was by steam and a screw propeller nineteen feet in diameter. On her sea trials she averaged almost seventeen knots, making her the fastest ship in the world. Her commanding officer reported her to ride well and to be "faultless." Many years later a marine historian stated that she was a magnificent success in every way, perhaps the greatest steam war vessel the world had ever seen.

Nonetheless, two years after her trials, a naval board recommended getting rid of the *Wampanoag,* and she was subsequently sold. The board maintained that she would not ride well because she did not fit the traditional design rules (she was judged too narrow in beam for her length). The fact that she actually proved seaworthy on her trials was ignored.

A more fundamental reason for the board's rejection, however, was fear of how steam vessels would change the navy's culture. As the board wrote in 1870,

> Lounging through the watches of a steamer, or acting as firemen and coal bearers, will not produce in a seaman that combination of boldness, strength and skill which characterized the American sailor of an elder day; and the habitual exercise

by an officer of command, the execution of which is not under
his own eye, is a poor substitute for the school of observation,
promptness, and command found only on the deck of a sailing
vessel.[12]

In their fears about the social impact of this new technology, the resisting naval officers were perceptive and correct.
The steam vessel did contribute to the reduction in the deck
officers' status and authority, but of course its dominance
over sailing ships was inevitable.

CHAPTER 9

Delegating More Clearly

"Why complain now? You should have asked what 'Special assistant to the President' meant before you took the job."

Poor delegation is one of the greatest causes of lost time. A subordinate is given an order. Thinking he understands, he accepts the obligation and charges off. But when the task is completed, all too often a disappointed superior realizes that the wrong job was performed because the subordinate didn't understand what was desired.

Delegating Power

The purpose of delegation is to transmit power from a superior to a subordinate so the latter can accomplish a necessary task.[1] It has its origins in the overworked owner–manager who could not keep up with everything and so hired someone to help him. Although he didn't give his new employee much authority or autonomy, he did have him assume some of his activities.

Much delegation in larger organizations shares this general theme: grudging assignment of tasks that the manager would prefer to do himself if only he had the time. And all time is not saved when a manager delegates. He still must supervise, monitor, and correct the subordinate, especially initially because the new person is not as competent as he is.

Some supervisors feel that they can do the job faster without a subordinate. In the short run they are probably correct. In the long run, however, delegation will enable the subordinate to develop competence and free the superior to devote time to longer-range matters. That is, the superior will be freer if he has delegated authority clearly enough so that the subordinate knows what to do and what is expected of him.

Ambiguous delegation. A recurring problem that wastes enormous chunks of time is that of the harried superior who doesn't take time to define what he expects and the inexperienced or fearful subordinate who doesn't ask the tough questions necessary to clarify the situation. Both parties should recognize that there are several forms of delegation.

And each should know what form is intended between them. For example, when superior A delegates to subordinate B, A should clarify what degree of initiative he expects from the subordinate.[2]

1. Look into this problem. Give me all the facts. I will decide what to do.
2. Let me know the alternatives available with the pros and cons of each. I will decide which to select.
3. Recommend a course of action for my approval.
4. Let me know what you intend to do. Delay action until I approve.
5. Let me know what you intend to do. Do it unless I say not to.
6. Take action. Let me know what you did. Let me know how it turns out.
7. Take action. Communicate with me only if your action is unsuccessful.
8. Take action. No further communication with me is necessary.

Clarity in initial instructions will save time and embarrassment. After the pattern is defined, the superior should adhere to it consistently until the delegated task is completed. Without such clarification and consistency, anxious subordinates may tend toward the first two patterns because they fear taking action for which they could be criticized. As a consequence, the superior will find herself continually consulted and possibly submerged in trivia.

President Eisenhower is said to have preferred delegation styles 3 and 4. He wanted his White House assistants to supply him with detailed proposals that he could approve and implement merely with a signature.[3] In contrast, President Kennedy favored forms 1 and 2; he wanted to be involved in early discussions developing the facts and generating alternatives (especially after the Bay of Pigs fiasco when he inadvertently delegated excessive power to the CIA).[4]

President Truman seemed to lean toward form 8—at least according to one high appointee who maintained that when he once tried to report on his activities, HST cut him short: "You're doing a good job. You'll hear from me when you're not. Now, let's talk about the Civil War."

President Nixon's style was less consistent. His critics maintained that he veered from no delegation or excessive withdrawal to the total delegation of forms 7 and 8. (Or as a cynic might attribute to Nixon, "Do it any way you can, but *don't* let me know about it!" A new form 9?)

One criticism leveled at President Carter early in his administration was that his intellectual skills were so great that he immersed himself in excessive detail *à la* delegation forms 1 and 2. According to one former aide, he even kept the schedule for the White House tennis courts.

Lack of delegation. Many owners, executives, and managers complain how overworked they are, but they will not delegate enough to lighten their burdens. Fear deters them. The manager may be afraid that a subordinate will not be able to perform the activity as well as *he* can. Therefore, he fears that his superior will be displeased with the results. Worse, an insecure manager may be anxious about his subordinate doing a better job thus threatening the manager's position.

More subtly, a manager may fear the ambiguity of not being continually on top of everything. Dependency on subordinates can provoke great anxiety in a manager who is averse to risk. This anxiety is especially great when the manager cannot define precisely what he wants the subordinate to do and therefore can't accurately measure how well it is being done.

This fear is understandable, but a manager who cannot stand the anxiety of delegation is fleeing from his managerial role. He ought to look for other work.

Failure to accept. Inadequate delegation is not always the superior's fault. Some subordinates resist delegation because they want to avoid anxiety, dislike their superior, or simply don't want to be bothered. Others may resist because they lack the self-confidence to stand criticism.

In addition, subordinates may not be offered sufficient

incentive to accept more than the most narrow task ("It's not *my* job!"). If forced to do more, they may repeatedly ask the boss for detailed instruction on each step. The superior may well conclude that he should not have bothered to try to delegate the task at all.

Pseudo Delegation

Actual delegation may be rarer than managers imagine. William Oncken suggests that many managers intend to delegate and even think that they do, but, somehow, the monkey of responsibility keeps jumping off their subordinates' shoulders and back onto their own.[5] Paradoxically, it may seem that delegating a task to a subordinate requires more of a superior's time than if he had performed the job himself. In fact, pseudo delegation occurs when a subordinate manipulates a superior into relieving him of responsibility for taking the next step in a delegated task. By making disguised demands on his boss's time, a subordinate may, in Oncken's view, even become his boss's boss.

Subordinate-imposed time demands. Such manipulation of a superior by a subordinate's apparently innocent requests might be called the "rubber-band effect." The analogy is obvious in the following common examples of a delegated job being snapped back to a superior by a subordinate.

1. *"We've got a problem."* Manager A greets one of his subordinates, B, while walking down the hall late for another meeting. B says, "Good morning. By the way, we've got a problem. The . . ." As B talks, superior A recognizes that he is not knowledgeable enough to make an immediate decision. To save immediate time so he can get on to his meeting, manager A responds, "Glad you brought this up. I'm in a rush right now. Let me think about it and I'll let you know."

In such an interaction, the subordinate has miraculously

relieved herself of responsibility for the next step. She only has to wait until her superior gets back to her. And in a manner, the subordinate has even more miraculously transformed herself into the superior because manager A now has the responsibility to do something and report back to B. Subordinate B may even "supervise" her superior by later asking how things are coming along on the problem.

2. *"Send me a memo."* Suppose that, at the end of a conference with subordinate C, manager A concludes, "Fine, send me a memo on that." The responsibility remains with the subordinate, but only until he sends the requested memo. Once the report leaves C's desk, the obligation for action jumps to manager A. Subordinate C will do nothing until he receives A's response to the memo (and may well grumble at A's slowness).

To push the boss along, subordinate C may well write another memo to A indicating that he needs a response soon. Once again, manager A is time-pressured and "supervised" by his own subordinate.

3. *"I'll draw up a discussion draft."* Consider the situation in which a new position has been created and subordinate D is brought in. Manager A has told her that they should get together soon to define the new job's objectives and that "I'll draw up an initial draft for discussion."

Once again, manager A has put himself into the position of making the next move. Subordinate D may spin her wheels until A produces the draft and calls for a meeting.

In each of these three incidents, Oncken maintains, the superior mistakenly assumes that the problems were "joint" when in fact he should ensure that they are primarily the subordinate's. Manager A has simply allowed too many "monkeys" to jump onto his shoulders. Pretty soon he will be working on Saturdays while subordinates B, C, and D are playing golf.

Keeping delegated jobs delegated. Managers should not allow themselves to be manipulated into relieving their subordinates of responsibility for the next step. The initiative for the next step should remain with the subordinate who should then report to the superior. When talking to a subordinate about a problem, the manager's self-reminder should be, "At no time while I am helping you with this will your problem become my problem. When this meeting is over, the problem will leave this office exactly the way it came in—on your back."

With regard to the three incidents described where responsibility was snapped back to the superior, perhaps manager A could have clearly directed the subordinate to take the next step:

1. With respect to "We've got a problem," A could tell B to come to his office later with the possible alternatives and her recommendation. Thus B must work until the decision is made, not A.
2. On "Send me a memo," A would be more time-efficient "single handling" the issue. If he understood C's problem, he should have made a decision right away. If not, he should have told C to proceed but to keep A informed. He would have minimized added delay from a written report.
3. On "I'll draw up a discussion draft," he shouldn't have. The superior should have the subordinate draw up the proposal for discussion at a time set by the superior.

Parallel to the forms of delegation I've described, Oncken suggests five degrees of initiative that a subordinate can exercise in relation to his superior.

Lowest Initiative	1. Wait until told
	2. Ask what to do
	3. Recommend
Highest Initiative	4. Act but advise at once
	5. Act on own, report later

Rather optimistically, Oncken suggests that no manager should use forms 1 and 2 or accept a subordinate who uses them. Subordinates should know that they must exercise more initiative and an effective manager defines the desired initiative level on each matter.

Rejection of initiative forms 1 and 2 seems a bit extreme.

Particularly ambiguous or risky projects may justify less subordinate initiative. Nonetheless, clarity of form is surely time-saving.

Delegating to Staff

Clarifying the nature of the authority delegated is particularly tricky with staff personnel. The classic view is that firms contain two kinds of units, line and staff, and that staff should have no authority to make decisions, only to advise.[6] If advisers give orders on their own, according to this view, unity of command is destroyed and confusion reigns. In practice, however, staff often is delegated substantial authority and for good reasons. We can distinguish between several kinds of staff and the authority delegated to them.

Personal staff. The simplest kind of staff is formed when an overworked manager engages an assistant to help him with his work. On the organization chart, such assistants would appear as a box to the side of the chain of command (see Figure 8). A personal staff assistant has no authority inde-

Figure 8. Personal Staff

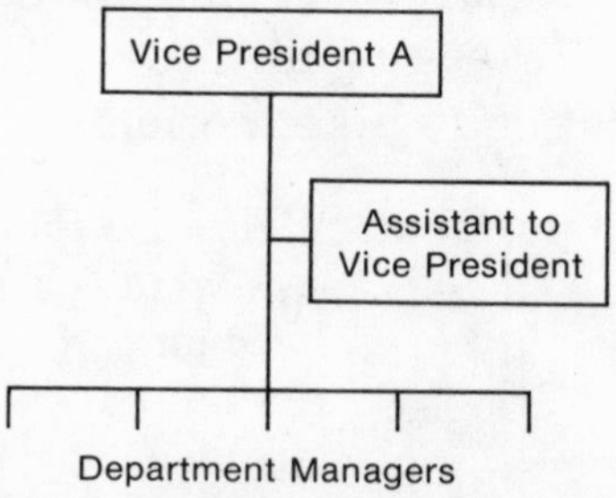

pendent of the executive. He or she is available to do whatever A wants him to: draw up complex documents or fetch coffee. Before anything the assistant recommends can be implemented, it must be approved by A. To ease the burden, some line executives authorize their assistants to sign their names so that lower personnel think a directive originates with the executive when in fact it comes from the assistant. This practice can be dangerous, however, because the executive may inadvertently abdicate his responsibilities to his personal staff.

Although a staff assistant may possess no formal authority, he can still exercise substantial influence. If subordinates perceive that A trusts assistant B, they may begin to court B hoping he will put in a good word for them with A. They may even go to B for instructions so that A is not bothered.

Advisory staff. Advisers are hired to take advantage of the contributions to company goals that specialization can make. These staff specialists will be consulted when line managers need advice, as in the interaction shown in Figure 9. In this flow of communication, staff possesses no authority

Figure 9. Advisory Staff

and only gives advice. A production manager may call an engineering specialist if he is having trouble maintaining his equipment, a manufacturing foreman may call a personnel specialist if he is having discipline problems with a particular worker, and so on.

Unfortunately, in spite of the framed diplomas they hang above their desks, newly hired staff specialists may find that they are not called for advice.[7] Rather they are instructed by their superiors to "sell" themselves to line managers, as illustrated in Figure 10. Such selling requires frequent, vigorous overtures to line management, a reverse of the behavior usually required of an adviser.

Figure 10.   Advisory Staff That Sells Itself

To engage in such selling, staff must have right of entry to line departments. Such a right cannot be assumed because some line managers forbid staff from entering if they can. A higher line executive may have to order line management to allow staff entry. To preserve the separation of line authority and staff advice, however, line management would have to remain free to reject staff proposals.

Figure 11.   Staff Authority

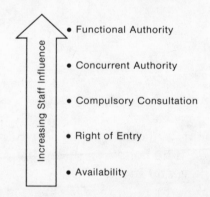

Top management may soon discover that hiring specialists, providing them with luxurious offices, and giving them right of entry into line departments does not guarantee that they will be heeded. To make sure that staff expertise is being used, management may delegate additional authority to staff. The staff can be strengthened by movement along the continuum of staff influence beyond availability and entry rights to compulsory consultation, concurrent authority, and functional authority as illustrated in Figure 11.

Compulsory consultation. To ensure that line consults staff on specific matters, top management may refuse to discuss lower line proposals unless staff has first been consulted. In the example illustrated in Figure 12, vice president B may

Figure 12. Compulsory Consultation Staff

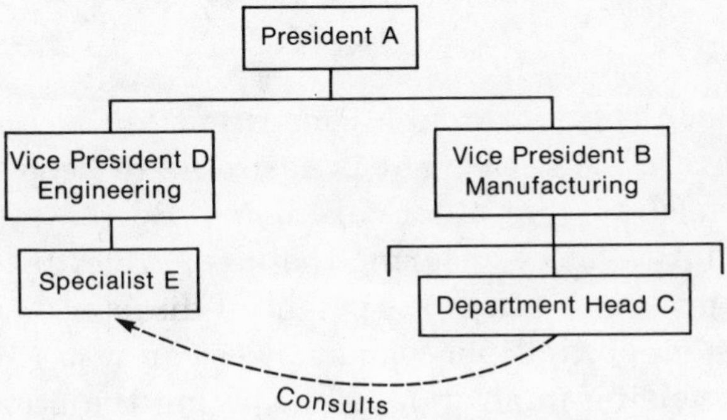

refuse to discuss department head C's request to replace manufacturing equipment until C has consulted with staff specialist E in the engineering division. President A insists on this to ensure that the engineering specialists have an opportunity to influence manufacturing methods.

Concurrent authority. If it wants to give staff a little more influence, top management may require staff approval of all line decisions. In effect, this gives a staff specialist veto power over a line manager if he disagrees with the manager's proposal. Figure 13 illustrates how president A may require that manufacturing obtain the concurrence of the industrial engineering department before scheduling overtime. Thus department head D will have to request that specialist F sign the overtime schedule, and this will serve as a check against poor planning and excessive overtime expense.

Figure 13.   Concurrent Authority Staff

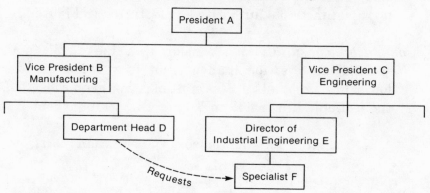

Such checks through concurrent authority are common in government, where it is desirable to keep many persons informed of what others are doing. Such a system can prevent mistakes by ensuring that every relevant specialist has his opportunity to block potential disasters. Unfortunately, a system of multiple concurrences can also lead to rejection of promising innovation. Multiplying the number of people who can say no probably reduces both errors *and* creative breakthroughs.

Functional authority.   Management can go so far in its staff support that the line—staff distinction is dissolved.[8] Each functional unit is assigned authority over set policies and procedures in its area of expertise. Thus, in Figure 14, the personnel V.P. may be responsible for all employment and training, the engineering V.P. for all product design, the director of industrial engineering for all production methods and incentive standards, and the financial V.P. for all cost control and accounting procedures. Each is supreme in his or her area as long as top management validates the decisions.

Functional authority ideally ensures that persons with expertise have authority in their areas, independent of ob-

Figure 14. Functional Authority Staff

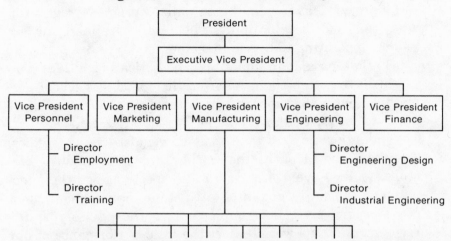

solete boundaries between staff and line.[9] Nonetheless, there are some problems. Widespread functional authority undermines the principle of unity of command, especially for line managers at lower and middle levels. So many functional officials can exercise influence that a line manager receives contradictory directives. And each function tends to see its responsibility as most important, even though all are equally important and dependent on each other. Coordination of these different functions is a top executive responsibility, but it is a difficult task.

No single location along the continuum of staff authority is ideal. It is a practical issue not a theoretical dispute. Management must balance the desire for high-level expertise and standardized plans against the advantages of lower-level control under the principle that authority should equal responsibility.

Ineffective Relations between Line and Staff

In spite of competent staff advisers, projects sometimes go awry. Line management feels that it can't use the advice offered by staff, and specialist hours and calendar time are lost. We can understand why projects go wrong by considering each party's point of view.[10]

Line management's view.   The staff members are so eager to sell a project that they make unrealistic promises regarding what they will be able to do. The results are more modest and disappointing to line management.

Staff proposals are sometimes theoretically brilliant (and might have gotten them A's from their business school professors), but unfortunately these theoretical answers don't apply to our particular problems.

The advisory staff tend to have very specialized views. Therefore they look at the world through their own telescopes. They have overly narrow perspectives and their recommendations are not integrated. Line management must consider, however, how implementing the advisory staff's recommendations would affect the total performance of our organization.

Advisory staff's view.   Line managers tend to blame the staff when projects don't work out. But they create many of the difficulties themselves. For example, a manager will toss a problem to us and expect an "answer" without his involvement. If we try to get him to spend time with us analyzing the issues, he complains that he called us to do that. In short, managers try to delegate the responsibility for projects to us without giving us either the necessary authority or personal support.

Line managers want improvement in their unit's performance without any change in their own personal behavior. They expect us to change the behavior of others while their own remains unchanged.

Sometimes a line manager will tell staff to give priority treatment to a project. After we have invested much time in it and have come back with recommendations, we find that the manager has lost interest in the project. His priorities changed and we were never informed. It all seems such a waste of time.

CHAPTER 10

Handling Role Stress

"You'd damn well better come up with an
antidote before five o'clock, Stimson. This project has cost
enough without having to pay you overtime."

Yes? No? More? Less? Go? Stay? Now? Later? Slow? Quick?
He? She? Black? White? Young? Old? New? Used? Lead?
Lag? Like Hamlet's sea of troubles, a multitude of decisions
presses on managers—decisions that become increasingly
complex and time-consuming. And there's the rub: time does
not grow with the expanding number, scope, and importance
of these decisions. Indeed, it seems to shrink. And with that
apparent shrinkage comes stress.

In Shakespeare's words, "All the world's a stage, and all
the men and women merely players" who are attempting to
fulfill the requirements of their various roles. Students may
also be sons or daughters, boyfriends or girl friends, athletes,
reporters, church members, or citizens. Professors may be
teachers, researchers, consultants, wives or husbands, mothers or fathers, community volunteers, or home mechanics. A
business executive may also be chairperson of the board of
trustees of the local hospital, area chair for college alumni,
vestryman at church, membership committee member at the
country club, and candidate for election to the county board.
Some of these roles are more enjoyable than others, but
nearly all generate certain stresses and strains.[1]

Causes of Role Stress

Each person is expected by his or her superiors, peers, subordinates, and others to behave in certain ways (called role
demands). These demands are made by the various people
with whom the person lives and works: those who collec-
tively comprise one's "role set."[2] Unfortunately, stress develops when the demands are inadequate, excessive,
contradictory, conflicting, or ambiguous.

Inadequate demand. Position demands are sometimes small
compared with the incumbent's capacity. This is the familiar
stereotype of the narrowly defined and programmed blue-
collar production job. Many young college graduates (especially women) also find that their first jobs do not challenge

them. Research on the strikingly low morale among engineers indicates that this condition is widespread.[3] Many organizations have graduate engineers performing activities that do not draw on their abilities and could be better performed by lesser educated technicians. Overeducation for American jobs is exceedingly common—so common that at each hierarchical level, those individuals with less education may have higher morale and perform just as effectively as those at the same level with greater education.[4]

Demand overload. A position can be much larger than the incumbent can handle. The person is performing to maximum capacity but cannot meet all the role demands. The popular Peter Principle maintains that everyone eventually faces this state.[5] Supposedly, we all rise to the level of our incompetence where role demands are just too large for us. The popularity of the concept suggests that it has some validity, but most of us probably use the "principle" to explain our superiors' problems—not our own. The major weakness in the idea is that it ignores the possibility of growth, for expanding demands can challenge the incumbent to grow. Harry Truman rose to the level of his incompetence, but then he seemed to develop into a competent (some say even outstanding) president. Somewhere there is a job that is beyond the grasp of almost everyone, but it is not necessarily in our hierarchy and we do not necessarily reach it.

Contradictory demands from one person. Even if only one person is making demands, an individual can confront inconsistency and contradiction. The demands may call for simultaneous behavior patterns that are impossible to combine. Mother expects little David to keep clean, straighten his room, study his school work, practice the piano, play with his friends, and complete household chores, all between 4:00 and 5:00 P.M.

Similar problems exist at work. Colleges frequently hire graduate students as dormitory advisers and expect them simultaneously to live with undergraduates and to be a friend and adviser to them, to be a communications link to the administration, and to be an enforcer of university regulations. However, it is difficult to be both friend and police officer. Being too conscientious in the latter role can destroy the former. Similarly, in industry some industrial engineers are expected to be advisers to line managers at the same time that they monitor production performance and set standards and budgets. Advising and monitoring are tough to combine because a person is unlikely to discuss his real inadequacies with anyone who evaluates him. Managers may not necessarily lie, but they sometimes hide the truth. This is the same reason that teenagers do not confide in their parents; they consult friends instead because talking truthfully to parents might destroy the ideal image that they want mother and father to hold of them.

Conflicting demands from several people. All members of a person's role set (especially one's superior) depend in some way upon one's performance; they are rewarded by it or they require it in order to perform their own tasks. Because they have a stake in one's performance, they develop various expectations about one's behavior. Unfortunately, these expectations do not always agree, so the role set imposes conflicting demands. The harried incumbent is compelled to demonstrate contradictory or inconsistent behavior. For example, university professors experience substantial role conflict. They are expected to teach, and pressure is increasing from students and administrators to do a better job; they are also expected to do research and to publish. In recent years, they also have been expected to assist in the solution of local and national social problems.

The classic business example of role conflict has been the production supervisor described as a "person in the middle" and a "victim of doubletalk."[6] He is caught between the declaration of his superiors that he is a member of management, the power residing in staff "advisers" who tell him what to do, and the pressures of former working companions who control much of his social satisfactions.

Managers occupying boundary positions, such as marketing managers who have extensive contacts with outsiders, work under role conflict. Some of their customers' expectations on delivery time, product quality, and credit terms may be inconsistent with company policies.[7] Nevertheless, corporate executives still expect the manager to compete.

Division general managers in large corporations occupy rewarding but stressful positions.[8] They must maintain three-way relationships—upward to corporate staff, laterally to other divisions, and downward to subordinates. Unfortunately, responding to one of these can undermine another. For instance, a middle manager who obediently follows orders from headquarters may thereby weaken her authority over her subordinates, who perceive her as a mouthpiece. Pushing the subordinates' interests too strongly, however, may lead the superiors to conclude that she has no overall perspective, or, even worse, that she is disloyal. Adding to the ambiguity is the fact that her responsibility almost always exceeds her authority. The middle manager is responsible for the performance of the division and the profits achieved, but sometimes corporate staff sets policies that she thinks are incorrect and that hinder the achievement of objectives.

Ambiguous or unknown demands. Perhaps the most stressful situation is when individuals do not know what is expected of them. Students dislike teachers who give no feedback on performance so that grades seem as if they were drawn from a hat. And managers complain when they cannot determine the criteria by which superiors are evaluating their performance.

All promotions carry some ambiguity stress, for the promoted manager must give up the comforting known for the sometimes threatening unknown.[9] Managers must acclimate themselves to new demands and learn new behaviors to perform their roles. To add to the difficulty, some of their old friends and peers may now be subordinates on whom the managers must depend for information and assistance. As managers move upward in status, pay, and power, they unexpectedly find themselves in increasingly dependent and ambiguous positions.

The problem of knowing who to play to and how to evaluate performance is widespread. Research on the early careers of young managers suggests that the central problems are ignorance or misunderstanding of the precise standards used to evaluate performance (that is, ignorance of real role demands), and insensitivity to the actual power structure in the organization (that is, confusion about the role set).[10]

Tactics for Handling Role Stress

The most debilitating response to role stress paradoxically is the most passive. The unfortunate person can respond by simply accepting the ambiguity and endeavoring to overcome it by working harder to meet everyone's expectations. Some great men and women may be all things to all people, but most cannot. Trying to meet all demands can have a markedly adverse impact on satisfaction and even on mental and physical health.[11] The time of one's life can be chewed up by others' inappropriate demands. But we are not helpless. We don't have to be passive. Tactics for handling role stress include flight, selective withdrawal, response to power, response to authority, compartmentalization of demands, and confrontation.

Flight. The most dramatic response to stress is to flee. Unpleasant, contradictory, or ambiguous demands are rendered irrelevant by fleeing the field of battle. It is tempting because it appears easy to drop out of school, quit a job, resign from a community position, or even flee from an incompatible spouse. But its simplicity is misleading, for no one can live in a vacuum. Complete escape from role demands is an impossibility short of hermitism, insanity, or death. People who habitually run from stress have a way of repeatedly finding themselves in similar stressful situations. Certainly resignation is a valid step for courageous people, but only when other devices will not work.[12]

Selective withdrawal. A person under stress may temporarily withdraw when stress builds up.[13] For example: "Every time we get a rush job he gets one of those headaches and has to go home." Or an individual may informally ignore some of the conflicting demands and avoid the persons imposing them. The dormitory adviser might avoid all communication with school administrators and quietly stop enforcing regulations. The professor may simplify his situation by teaching as little as possible and literally hiding from students. The aim of withdrawal is to reduce and simplify role demands. A naval officer's comments are typical:

> The Executive Officer's job was to check on my performance. I never liked having to respond to him. . . . I soon decided that to maintain my equilibrium I should avoid interaction with him if at all possible. I made it a habit to spend prolonged periods of time down in the hot engine rooms where he was unlikely to follow—and I never went for coffee in the ward room.

Rather than totally ignoring a person, it is possible to compromise by responding only to exceptionally important demands. Thus the competitive elements of conflicting demands can be played down. The dormitory adviser might take action against major rule violations only and ignore the more numerous minor ones. The newly promoted supervisor might apply pressure on former working buddies only when a crisis arises or when higher management is physically present. Otherwise the supervisor adheres to the group's informal code.

Response to power. The most pragmatic response to conflicting demands from various people is to minimize pain. Give priority to the person who can reward or punish the most. In an organization this is likely to be some superior. The problem with this criterion is that it is not always easy to determine who really has the most power. And even if this is possible, responding only to him or her can still hurt because others may also possess power which can be used in retaliation for ignoring their demands. Finally, such a self-centered rule will adversely affect relations with the respondent's lateral associates and subordinates. They may feel that they have been sold out.

Even the boss may not be entirely satisfied if giving him priority means the role is not performed well. One study indicates that the lowest rated supervisors conformed the most to direct superiors, while higher rated managers ignored demands that interfered with performance.[14] They get the job done, and this is what superiors value most.

Response to authority.   Another pragmatic solution is to give priority to the demands that are judged most legitimate. The question asked is who has the most right to the results of your role performance. Power and authority may reside in the same superior, but this is not always the case. A powerful vice president may bypass your department head to order you to concentrate on project B, while your direct boss wants project A completed first. The most legitimate demand is probably the department head's, but the vice president has more power.

The conflict between power and authority can be particularly acute where powerful figures want the individual to exploit others or to violate the law. An unfortunate manager might see his career blocked unless a subordinate is wrongfully fired, a competitor illegally spied upon, or a pollution statute broken. A morally sensitive person may know what is right in such rare circumstances, but the choice will still be unpleasant either way.

Compartmentalization of demands.   A person can develop arbitrary personal rules that separate demands and that are followed even when not exactly appropriate to a unique situation. For example, a professor might devote Tuesdays and Thursdays wholly to her classes and students; Mondays and

Wednesdays she might research and write; Fridays she could engage in community service or pursue extra income. Note that the intent of such arbitrary rules is to simplify the professor's life. She does not have to decide what to do with each demand; she just fits it into a category.

Similarly, an executive might allot three nights a week to his family, regardless of job demands, and never depart from this pattern. Or he may unquestionably work late when his superior demands it, regardless of his son's basketball game. The advantage of such impersonal rules is that one does not have to analyze the specific situation before applying the prescription.

Confrontation.   The healthiest (and more courageous) response to role stress is to attempt to modify others' demands through confrontation and bargaining.[15] The misassigned individual could apply for a transfer; the underchallenged could request more interesting work; the overwhelmed could demand a relaxation of the pressure. Similarly, the person experiencing role conflict could inform the superiors that they should coordinate or simplify their expectations. The college dormitory adviser could ask to be relieved of his or her police duties; the professor could request evaluation as a teacher *or* researcher, but not both; the supervisor could ask for a transfer to a department where he or she is not supervising friends; the division general manager can ask central corporate staff to rescind undesired policies; and spouses can agree to change their expectations of each other. Especially when accepting a delegated task, a subordinate should request that his superior clarify the nature of the delegation as we discussed in Chapter 9.

Unfortunately many managers and professionals are characterized by personal passivity. Huge gobs of calendar and career time are lost because they don't attempt to change others' demands.[16]

Passivity sometimes springs from a feeling of helplessness—the organization has so many confining rules and traditions that you can't be "different." To behave differently than those others might be dangerous because "one simply doesn't do that." Of course, organizations demand substantial conformity, but some management observers suggest that many binding chains are of our own forging and that many organizations would accept and reward initiative.[17] Thus, a young assistant manager in a department store was told by everyone that he wouldn't be allowed to sell used jeans. Their affluent clientele would be offended and it would anger store management. But he did and no one was. His initiative was very successful and he was widely praised.

It is always easier to drift with the times and hope things will work out for the best, but this is not a recipe for managerial success. The paradox is that it is the most promising young men and women who find it easiest to drift. To be in demand is a mark of status and being busy gives a feeling of importance. Consequently, a talented young person might allow himself to be dominated by others' desires.

Unfortunately for the person experiencing stress, the people imposing the undesired demands may be unwilling to modify them. Whether their reasons for refusal are valid or not is quite irrelevant if they believe in them. Consequently, requesting change requires some courage, and to push too hard can be foolish. An individual who initiates a talk with his or her spouse about changing their marriage relationship can deeply offend the other party. An organizational superior will probably listen to a subordinate who respectfully requests a change, and no retaliation will result. The boss may not make the change, however. And if the subordinate becomes too insistent, the superior may feel angry and threatened, so much so that she may punish the person who rocks the boat.

In his approach to time management, Alec Mackenzie suggests that managers learn how to say no to their superiors by encouraging subordinates to say no to them.[18] Many managers are horrified at the idea, but consider his point. Certainly a manager has a right to expect that his or her subordinates will generally do what they are told. Sometimes, however, a subordinate has an obligation not to do what a superior directs.

Newton Minow was director of the Federal Communications Commission under President Kennedy. One evening Kennedy became extremely angry after watching the "Huntley–Brinkley" news report. He felt they had unjustly criticized him. In a fit of rage, he called Minow on the telephone and with various colorful oaths ordered his aide to punish NBC, to "get" those S.O.B.s by any means available.[19] Minow replied that he would look into it.

But Minow did nothing. The next day he wrote a note to Kennedy indicating how lucky the president was to have subordinates who were so loyal that they didn't always do what they were told. Kennedy recognized Minow's wisdom and called him with thanks. Minow believed, and Kennedy agreed (when his anger had abated), that a loyal subordinate sometimes should say no in order to protect his boss from the consequences of his own folly.

Saying no extends to telling a superior that his time demands are excessive or his deadlines impossible to meet. That does not mean the subordinates refuse to perform the tasks. Rather, subordinates should bargain with their superiors with respect to unreasonable demands. Don't passively accept a deadline when you know meeting it will be impossible. To remain silent will mislead the superior into thinking the job will be done on time.

The obligation sometimes to say no to your superiors gives you the courage to tell your subordinates to say no to you sometimes—to "manage you," in Mackenzie's phrase. As a superior, you must not abdicate in favor of your subordinates, but you should at least be receptive to their questioning of your time demands. You should be willing to bargain with your subordinates on these matters just as you sometimes want to negotiate with your superior.

All this saying no and bargaining is easier said than done, of course. Substantial courage and self-control are required. An astute manager will fight to change role demands, but not always. For example, a division general manager should oppose the most crippling central policies, but he cannot fight all the time, or his influence upward will be totally expended and his credibility gone. Like an army general, he battles only on the most favorable grounds.[20]

CHAPTER 11

Tactics for Survival

In the long run, effective time management means dealing with yourself at the most intimate level. As Walt Kelly's immortal Pogo exclaimed, "We have met the enemy and they is us!"

Transcending time is of course literally impossible short of Nirvana. Nonetheless, tactics exist for reducing one's personal dominance by the past and present. There are strategies for staying alive and being able to confront the future. We shall consider some of these tactics and strategies in this chapter.

James McCay's Quarterly Objectives

Habit and preoccupation are the central causes of wasted time according to James McCay.[1] As we master our jobs and grow older, we tend to behave without thinking. We sort of sleepwalk through our organizational lives allowing our perceptive skills to atrophy. Consequently, McCay argues, we should endeavor to increase our alertness and ability to concentrate.

Experience can be a great source of learning of course. It can certainly save a lot of time as we fit current problems into the learned categories from the past. Unfortunately, it can also waste time and cause disaster if we categorize prematurely and erroneously.[2]

Richard Nixon was regarded as one of the most effective personal time managers among modern presidents. Friends and enemies alike, however, wondered at the bungling of the Watergate episode. He seemed so cool and rational with respect to foreign policy, but he was inept and emotional in dealing with his biggest domestic crisis. Why the contradiction?

No one knows the ultimate answer of course, but a plausible explanation is improper categorization. Nixon seemed to perceive Watergate as a political issue not as an important domestic policy or moral matter. He believed that after some temporary flack the hubbub would die down as people lost interest in the affair. The "political" cue mentally filed the issue into a slot that activated the inappropriate response. Nixon seemed incapable of seeing Watergate deeply and uniquely until it was too late.

You have heard of people who have worked for twenty years, but don't have twenty years' experience. They merely repeated the first year twenty times. Such people may treat a new problem as if it were like problems in the past when it is really different. McCay, therefore, offers some tactics to avoid this error.

McCay suggests that for each three-month period we set three kinds of personal objectives: innovation, growth, and maintenance objectives.

Innovation objectives. Each quarter you should focus on one major aspect of your job and put it on trial for its life. It could be one of Joseph Trickett's "activities" or one of Alec Mackenzie's "responsibility categories." But it should be something central and important to your work.

This work aspect should be cross-examined to justify its existence. Could it be eliminated? If not, could it be modified and improved? Could it be delegated to someone else? In applying this tactic to my own work, for example, the task that jumps out at me is grading. After fifteen years as a teacher, I am experiencing increasing difficulty in evaluating student papers. This past semester was the first ever in which I assigned no Fs or D's! And I gave only five C's. The hundred other marks were B's and A's. Have I become too lax? Have I been corrupted by the grading inflation that infects schools everywhere? Or am I such an outstanding teacher that all my students are able to master the topic?

I would like to answer the last question affirmatively, but McCay's approach warns me that I should probe deeper. Perhaps I should change the format of my tests. I give only cases and essay questions, which require students to write fairly lengthy reports. But grading such reports is quite subjective. It is difficult sometimes to defend my judgment when an ambitious student complains. Perhaps I should consider changing my method. Other professors use a more objective true–false or multiple choice format. Such tests are much easier to grade and seem to provide more defensible numbers as grades.

This specific example of my personal grading problem is obviously not important to most readers, but the point is that we all have central aspects of our jobs on which we experience difficulty. These might benefit from becoming the focus of innovation for a quarter. In fact, my problem may also be common among managers. I recently conducted a survey among managers in a large conglomerate in which they had to indicate the most difficult aspects of their jobs. Their answer was that telling a senior subordinate that he or she is doing an unsatisfactory job is very hard, especially if the subordinate is older than the manager doing the rating. McCay's approach suggests that these managers might focus on their personal handling of performance evaluation asking these critical questions: can it be eliminated? can it be improved? can it be delegated?

If the problem with the work activity examined is not corrected in the three-month period, continue it as the innovation objective for the next quarter. If the problem is solved, take the rest of the quarter off. But find a new innovation objective for the next period.

Growth objectives. McCay's quarterly growth objectives have three dimensions: reading, daily practice, and interests requiring close observation.

You should plan your professional reading and not grab something near your desk as you leave for a plane (or worse, scan the paperback racks at the airport). The reading should be varied. Ambitious and devoted people tend to focus their reading too narrowly on their own fields. As a consequence, they are not encouraged to lift their thinking to higher levels. And they don't have creative ideas because most creativity doesn't spring fully defined from the creator's mind. Rather most creativity consists of borrowing something from one context and applying it to another. Research on creative scientists suggests that they have a wide range of information sources. [3]

Daily practice of a skill requiring close observation is the central aspect of McCay's growth objective. Learning how to play the piano at age 35, or starting to paint at age 45, or studying a foreign language at 55 are all vehicles for keeping alive the ability to perceive uniquely. Daily practice will cause you to give up the comfortable known and confront the unknown. In this confrontation it is less important that you actually master the new than that you give it a good effort.

Maintenance objectives.   The final quarterly target is one improvement that you will make over the next three months in either your diet, physical activity, or recreation. What can you do at the most personal behavioral level to improve your well-being?

In raising this question, McCay sounds a little like Saint Francis or Benjamin Franklin. He asserts that mastering your own eating, exercise, and play habits will provide a tonic to your total life situation. Being in control of yourself at this level will permeate your life, spill over onto the job, and improve your sense of mastery.

My own first application of this quarterly objective led to the virtual elimination of soft drinks from my diet. Long a cola freak (since I don't drink coffee, I had to find something to keep me awake in college and the navy), I consumed about six cans a day. That is a lot of refined sugar! The reduced sugar intake was desirable and the twenty-pound weight loss rewarding, but even more beneficial was the verification that I could do it. This is McCay's central thesis on maintenance objectives.

The major purpose of all of McCay's tactics is to help you perceive situations as unique, to retain your ability to see how the present is different from the past, and how the future will be different still. He wants you to retain a tolerance for ambiguity.

Note that McCay's idea brings us full circle from Peter Drucker's central definition of a manager as a person able to

see the general in a series of seemingly unique events. Thus
for Drucker, as we discussed in Chapter 6, a key managerial
skill is converting unique, crisis events into patterned, routine behavior. Drucker is correct for most of an organization's activities and management's time, but McCay warns
us of the dangers in becoming too proficient at categorizing.
He wants us to retain the nonmanagerial, artistic skill of
perceiving profoundly and uniquely.

Alan Lakein's Life Control

The best-selling time management book has probably been
Lakein's *How to Get Control of Your Life and Time.*[4] Surprisingly, it says very little about work. The focus is on life
off the job. However, Lakein's implicit assumption is that
achieving a sense of control over one's personal life will have
an impact on one's work performance.

Lakein prescribes a very specific approach to generating
"lifetime goals." Movement toward these goals is important;
compulsively keeping track of where your minutes are going
is not. Hence he begins with a warning to "beware the time
nut" who maintains time diaries or logs (so much for
Drucker and Mackenzie!). The steps in Lakein's approach
include (1) generating lifetime goals; (2) specifying activities
to accomplish the goals; and (3) scheduling and performing
the activities.

Lifetime goals.   A six-step exercise involving three lists is suggested for generating lifetime goals.

1. Label a blank sheet of paper, "What are my lifetime goals?"
    Then write as fast as you can, not in priority order, but as
    the thoughts occur. Include ambitions that might seem pre-
    posterous such as "become president of the company," or "go
    to dentistry school," or even "become a saint." What is im-
    portant is to tap your basic dreams. Write for three minutes,
    then take three more minutes to clarify thoughts and messy
    handwriting. Put this first list aside.

2. Label a second sheet, "How would I like to spend the next five years?" Again, write rapidly for three minutes, suspending priority judgment or censorship. Write even if your thoughts include less than admirable desires like "chase show girls in Atlantic City" or "life guards at Malibu." Both would probably be exhausting if acted upon, but the intention here is to be truthful with yourself. After three minutes of generating this second goal list, take three more minutes to clarify. Then set this second sheet aside also.
3. Label a third sheet, "If I knew I would be struck dead by a bolt of lightning six months from today, how would I live until then?" Write for three minutes and clarify for another three.
4. Check and revise all three lists, eliminating duplications.
5. Begin setting priorities by identifying the three most important goals on each list.
6. From the resulting nine life-goals, select the three you consider most important.

You might repeat the whole exercise several times over a couple of weeks until you have two lists, one with the nine goals and one with the final three, that you feel comfortable with. You might also plan on repeating the exercise on appropriate dates like your birthday or anniversary.

The three lists of ever nearer deadlines are intended to focus your thinking and to encourage you to be increasingly honest with yourself as to what is ultimately important to you (even if, and perhaps especially if, it appears trivial to others). For most people, therefore, the exercise must be private and confidential.

Specifying activities. As the old Chinese aphorism states, "The longest journey begins with a single step." The steps for accomplishing life-goals are activities to be performed in the present and near future. Lakein suggests the following for specifying these activities:

1. Write each of the three most important goals on separate sheets of paper.
2. For each of the three goals, list all possible activities that logically would contribute to goal achievement. If "take oil painting lessons" is one of your goals (as it was for me),

activities might include telephone calls or library research to locate a teacher, determine costs per lesson or course, find out whether costs are covered by veterans' benefits, and so on.

3. Begin to set priorities on activities by putting each to the question, "Am I committed to spending at least five minutes on this within the next seven days?" If the answer is no, cross out the activity.

You should thus prune your three activity lists down to a combined list of about twelve that you are willing to act upon in the near future.

Sophisticated psychology is operating here. Although some readers may feel the exercises are simplistic, they do draw you in. The progression develops involvement and determination to follow through.

Scheduling and performing activities.   As another old saying (of supposed American origin) goes, "You can lead a horse to water, but. . . ." So it is with these lists of life-goals and activities. To accomplish the goals, present time must be devoted to performing the activities. Lakein also gives advice on how to follow up on these priorities.

1. Set a deadline for each of the approximately twelve most important activities within the next seven days.
2. Block out time for activities that require more than a few minutes.
3. Every evening, look over the activities list and identify what you will do tomorrow.
4. Each day put at least one activity on your "to do" list and do it.
5. Periodically recheck your two lists of nine and three lifetime goals; generate additional activities as you perform them or as you learn more about what is necessary to accomplish a goal.

Central to Lakein's approach is confrontation and momentum. Alec Mackenzie's executive time inventory described in Chapter 6 forces its user to confront the discrepancy between his or her "ideal" time allocation and the reality of actual time expenditure on the job. The user continually has to make decisions on whether and what to do. Lakein wants you to confront your life-goals and make a daily decision to act upon them.

Daily action is an investment that will give you confidence in whatever you do. Healthy selfishness is involved here because you may be able to handle the inevitable boredom and purposelessness that characterizes at least part of all work *if you know that you will spend some time of the day on your own life-goals*. Progress toward those goals as indicated by activity accomplishment may create a sense of mastery that enables you to perform even better in all your various roles as employee, parent, and citizen.

The steps in the Lakein approach are clear and easy to initiate. One may question, however, whether the life-goal lists are valid. Many people may not be in touch with themselves enough to write down what is really important. They may be so subconsciously haunted by parental admonitions and by their Freudian superego that they internally censor their true desires. More profound counseling or psychotherapy may be required for some people to even begin thinking about self-goals—especially if, like some traditionally reared women, they have been taught to respond rather than to assert themselves.

A final possible criticism is that the approach runs the risk of glorifying narcissism and perhaps immorality. Not every goal is socially desirable and the approach seems devoid of moral guidelines. Certainly one of the central dilemmas of modern times is discovering a healthy balance between self-centeredness and self-sacrifice. Overemphasis on the self leads to social anarchy; overemphasis on others to a loss of individuality.

Exercises to Overcome Time Anxiety

Some psychotherapists (and marathon runners) argue that the best way to overcome fear and pain is to confront them head on. According to this view, one can master pain by welcoming it and transcending it. Or one can overcome a phobia by practicing small encounters with it.[5] Some behavioral psychologists, for example, help those who are fearful of flying by guiding them through a series of escalating encounters. First, merely a trip to the airport, then home. Second, to the airport and actually walking through the security check toward the departure gate; then home. Third, actually boarding a plane and sitting down, but deplaning before takeoff. Only in the fourth or fifth encounter would the person actually fly.

The aim of such scenarios is to help people to confront their fears and pain, to take some of the strangeness away. The approach may offer something for time-haunted, achievement-oriented people. Their fault is that they are too rooted in the present and short-run future, too impatient for feedback, and too busy *doing* things. More ambiguous and longer-term matters are dealt with only when they reach the present as emergencies.

Certain simple exercises may assist you to confront time. Try any or all of the following ten.

1. When waiting for your airplane to begin loading, don't rush to the gate immediately after the announcement to board your row. Rather, sit and wait until most other passengers have boarded. Your seat is reserved; there is no point in rushing ahead.

2. Similarly, when deplaning, don't bounce out of your seat even before the jet has pulled up to the gate. Sit in your seat and enjoy the rather silly spectacle of fellow passengers jostling each other in order to save three minutes (and not even that if they have checked luggage to fetch).

3. Extend this practice to other settings. Don't leave the ball game in the eighth inning or the concert in the middle of the last selection in order to "beat the crowd." You can be the last one out of the theater. You will lose very little actual time and it will feel luxurious.

4. As you approach a bridge toll station, don't frantically and dangerously shift lanes seeking the shortest line. Rather accept the line most convenient, even if it is the longest. While crawling to the gate, observe the people in the cars around you.

5. Except of course under exceptional circumstances, do not run to catch your bus or subway train even if walking might increase your chance of missing it. If you do miss it, you could have an unexpected tidbit of time, a gift that might be used. At the very least, you will feel more civilized.

6. Don't exceed the highway speed limit. Driving at 55 miles per hour not only is the law but also greatly facilitates noticing what you are driving by. And while commuting, you might occasionally drive a different, perhaps longer and less trafficked route. It will be a small adventure that relaxes the tension of elapsed travel time.

7. Walking or bicycling can have the same beneficial effect (in addition to health advantages). Awareness of the slower transportation mode can encourage you to plan ahead for adequate time to reach your destination. Allowing more time tends to reduce the feeling of time pressure.

8. If you are a boat person, sail instead of power cruising. Sailing puts you in touch with the weather and natural forces that elicit modesty about human power. And sailing forces you to confront time, to accept that certain activities just can't be hurried.

9. Perform household chores in an old-fashioned manual way. Hand-washing the dishes can be a satisfying experience once in a while (you really have to pay attention or you break them!).

10. Don't wear your watch on weekends. Not having your watch on your wrist will make it impossible to consult it continually as time-anxious people are inclined to.

The point of these trivial-appearing suggestions is to train yourself to reject slavery to time's tyranny in life's small aspects. You don't always have to hurry up and wait. Fighting time is a habit that can be broken. Plenty of big time pressures exist about which you can do little. Controlling the small things, however, can permeate your whole life just like McCay's quarterly objectives and Lakein's life-goals make big problems seem more manageable.

CHAPTER 12

Time and Success

"I'll never make it . . . I suffer from acrophobia."

An individual's attitudes toward time and career are not static. We all change with maturation and life phases. Therefore we need to examine these changes and how they affect personal "success" in managing time and career.

Personal Needs and Managerial Success

Many managers have a high need for achievement. The rigorous self-standards and orientation toward moderately risky activity leads to behavior that most employers reward. In small businesses, a direct relationship exists between achievement need and level: the person at the top has the highest need for achievement.

The picture in large firms may be a little different, however. In this setting, achievement need brings promotions only to a point near the upper portion of the middle management. Those who make the transition to the top appear to have somewhat lower achievement needs—still high with respect to most people but lower than many other managers and professionals. [1]

Several interpretations of this finding are possible: (1) the top executives are older and achievement need may decline with age and success; (2) the people at the top got there through connections rather than performance; or (3) needs other than achievement are central to making a successful transition to the top levels. The first two explanations may be partially valid, but the third one appears to be the most promising to explore.

Affiliation-oriented managers. Needs for affiliation, power, and achievement have been examined with reference to managerial success. One study asked superiors and subordinates to rate each manager on desirability and promotability. [2] Managers who are primarily affiliation-oriented don't work out well. There is consensus on this: subordinates don't like working for them and superiors don't rate them as promotable.

Such managers seem to be dominated by a short-run concern for pleasing people and being liked. Then talking with a subordinate, they seek a position that will leave both happy. But such a short-range outlook often backfires because of inconsistency and perceived inequity. Tomorrow the manager may reach a different conclusion on a similar matter with another subordinate who behaves more aggressively. Then yesterday's subordinate may feel cheated.

To be an effective manager requires transcending the present event to see it in the long run. You shouldn't make decisions just to satisfy the present moment without anticipating how the decision will affect others in the future.

Achievement-oriented managers. The predominantly achievement-oriented manager does not fare much better. Subordinates tend to see him as an undesired superior. Higher executives may like his performance, but they do not judge him as promotable. The problem seems to be that poor political skills handicap moving out of the technical ranks and up through management.

People who are intensely achievement-oriented often work poorly with others because of impatience with lower performance standards. A test that measures an "Index of Machiavellianism" has been developed to give a rough idea about interpersonal attitudes. Contrary to the test's name, power need is related less to the index than is achievement need. People with a high achievement need seem to view others as "objects" to be manipulated in the interest of their own accomplishment. Not that the achievement-oriented person dislikes others; this is simply irrelevant. What counts is getting those others to behave in the interest of the achievement. Not surprisingly, most subordinates dislike such impersonal and manipulative behavior.

Business students seem to have fairly high indices of Machiavellianism—higher than most managers (but not as high as business school professors!).[3] Managers have observed that many graduates take two or three years to learn that they must relate to other people as people not as resources or objects.

Power-oriented managers. Predominantly power-oriented managers seem to be more successful. They are better liked by subordinates and more likely to be promoted by superiors. The reason is not firmly established, but we could surmise that they have different perspectives on time and people. To satisfy one's power need requires insight into other people who are seen not so much as objects to be manipulated but as complex human beings to be influenced.[4] Actual feelings for them may be no warmer than those of the achievement-oriented manager, but the power seeker's behavior is more sophisticated. Time perspectives are longer-run and more directed to the viability of the system. A person with such an orientation is better able to climb through middle management into the conceptual policy-making ranks.

Personal Styles and Managerial Success

Another approach defines four types of executives: (1) organization man; (2) craftsman; (3) jungle fighter; and (4) gamesman (the types also apply to women, of course).[5] Figure 15 summarizes these categories in parallel to human need orientations.

Figure 15.   Manager's Need and Style Orientations

The organization man. This type is directed toward security and loyalty to the company. Safety and affiliation needs probably predominate. Such a person is unlikely to climb very high above entry ranks except in very stable institutions that value seniority.

The craftsman. Such a person is concerned mainly about quality task performance. Emphasis is on high standards and timely completion. Needs for competence and achievement are logically linked to this orientation. Such a manager is valued and promoted early in a career but is unlikely to make the transition to the top. Self-centeredness and political insensitivity block advance.

The jungle fighter. Jungle fighters used to climb to the top but are less likely to do so now. Their power orientation is strong and their influence is cultivated through dominance or manipulation. However, too open a power orientation is no longer popular. Because of organizational complexity, purely authoritarian styles are of declining effectiveness, especially at top levels.

The gamesman. The most successful executive seems to be the "gamesman" who is moderately high in both power and achievement needs. High performance standards are tempered by recognition of political realities. People skills rest on sufficient technical ability and conceptual thinking visualizes the long-run and larger system. Affiliation and status are less important—so much so that some observers express concern about executives' deferred affiliative needs and underexpressed emotions.[6]

In explaining why he left a senior executive post at Ford Motor Company to become president at Bell and Howell, Donald Frey catches the gamesman orientation:

> I just have to run a *whole* business—it's in here [he clutches his abdomen]. In the crudest sense, you could say it's a need for power. In an esoteric sense, it's a need for completeness. I'm not happy unless I'm dealing with all the pieces. All through

the years, regardless of what function I was performing, I had a desire to find out the broader aspects of what I was doing—to see what the next guy was going to do. [7]

Career Stages and Time Perspectives

Daniel Levinson has described six stages in a person's life and career. [8]

1. *Ages 16–22: Pulling up roots.* For most young people, a central concern is breaking away and establishing independence and autonomy, particularly from parents. They are concerned with proving to themselves that they are competent to make their own way. Consequently, jobs tend to be perceived as immediate vehicles for income and self-support rather than as introduction to careers.

2. *Ages 22–29: Provisional Adulthood.* The formation of intimate relationships is a central concern. These relationships are oriented toward other people, especially the opposite sex, but also include the development of ties with organizations and/or professions. Career success as a goal takes on added value.

3. *Ages 29–32: A transition period.* Uneasiness about progress tends to be common at this stage. Many worry if they are in the right place, or if they are headed in the desired direction fast enough. Shifting jobs and organizations is common because this group is becoming aware of the fact that personal mobility will begin to decline in the not distant future.

4. *Ages 32–39: Settling down.* For career-oriented, ambitious people, this period is marked by enormous concentration on work, advancement, and creativity. As a consequence, social contacts tend to be reduced as compared with earlier activity. For many, career and family activities leave little additional time for other relationships.

5. *Ages 39–43: Potential mid-life crisis.* At this stage, mobility begins to decline for most people. They begin to recognize that many youthful ambitions will never be fulfilled and that this may be the last time for fruitful evaluation of career progress and change of direction.

6. *Ages 43–50: Reestablishing and flowering.* Once the critical issues of commitment to a career have been handled satisfactorily, this stage suggests an optimistic stabilization

and contentment in relationships. Ambition is not forgotten, but is somehow transcended by many middle-aged people. They might still like to be vice president but have come to realize that it is not everything in life; that relationships within the organization at their present level can be developed and deepened.

Career stages and performance. Figure 16 parallels career stages with a subjective measure of personal "performance." This performance is not so much job effectiveness as it is an individual's sense of used potential—of firing all cylinders.

Figure 16. Career and Growth Stages

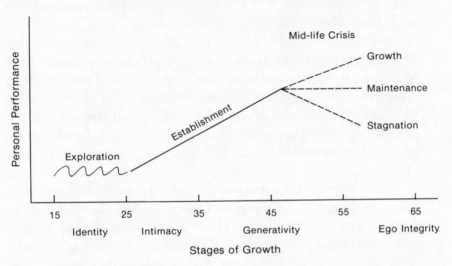

The critical problem of the late twenties and early thirties is commitment to a career and/or institution. Job and even career changes are frequent during this time.

If a young person is successful in connecting with a situation in which he or she feels comfortable, the period of the thirties and early forties is one of growth. For most successful people, this is the time of greatest sense of expansion. Task competence, promotions, rewards, and new challenges become part of life for the lucky and successful.

Some, of course, move faster than others. A study of presidents and executives divided them into three categories:

Table 5. Vertical Mobility of Managers

Level	Supermobiles	Normals	Submobiles
	years	*years*	*years*
Entrance job (technical)	1–2	2–3	3–4
Development (middle manage-ment)	11	14	15
Arrival (executive manage-ment)	8	10	17
Time to presidency	21	27	36

supermobiles, normals, and submobiles.[9] Table 5 summarizes the times spent at each level. Note that the supermobiles usually spend less than two years in the entrance job and that they change positions about every two years throughout the climb to the top. More common "normals" generally remain in the entrance position less than three years with approximately that interval between position changes. The supermobiles spend some eleven years in middle management and those who make it all the way to the presidency spend approximately eight years in the executive ranks. For normals, it is fourteen and ten years, respectively.

Rate of position moves is apparently an important indicator of progress. If your employer begins leaving you in positions much longer than three years, it may suggest some questioning of your fast-track potential. If the time climbs over five years, it may suggest that you have reached your plateau.[10]

These frequent position changes are not necessarily, or even usually, intercompany moves. The long-term trend in the United States during the twentieth century has been promotion from within. Such a policy varies with industries because some, such as advertising and television, demonstrate higher interfirm movement than the more stable banks and manufacturing concerns—at least after the first few years at work. About 25 percent of the top executives at the latter firms will have worked only for that company since graduation, but the other 75 percent will have had other jobs. Most of these jobs, however, were early in a career, mainly in the managers' twenties. Around age thirty, most of the climbers had joined the organization in which they made their ascent. As a general rule, changing firms before thirty years of age doesn't hurt (unless it is really excessive, suggesting inability to discipline oneself to work); mobility in the thirties can be risky unless it is clearly a promotion in opportunity to exercise autonomy and demonstrate performance (not just for more money); and mobility after forty-five is relatively difficult with the exception of organizations needing someone with your experience who is not available internally.

Generativity versus stagnation. Time works its inexorable will, however, and even the most successful people encounter unexpected problems in their middle forties—the so-called midlife crisis.[11] The issue is one of generativity and it revolves around whether repeating the past pattern will continue to be satisfying.[12] Unfortunately, for most of us it will not.

Several factors conspire to hinder simple repetition of the past as a source of satisfaction.

- We are a youth-oriented society so that as a manager moves into the late forties and fifties he or she may be perceived as less "promising." Younger people are seen as more promotable even though the fifteen years remaining in a fifty-year-old's career actually leave plenty of time for growth.
- The nature of organizational pyramids is such that a squeeze occurs near the top. Unless a firm is rapidly expanding, insufficient openings exist to keep up the rate of promotion experienced earlier in a career.
- We may lose some of our personal flexibility and courage in confonting new challenge. The genius of effective upwardly mobile managers is not that they do any single task better, but that have an ability to give up what they know, confront the unknown, master it, and perform effectively—and then repeat the whole cycle again and again.

Thus it is not that most people's performance deteriorates with age but that many if not most become increasingly reluctant to give up the known and confront the unknown. To do so requires physical energy and moral courage of which we may have only a limited supply.

If we attempt to just stay put but do a competent job on what we know, we may or may not be satisfied. The pessimistic view is that this won't work; that the task will become trivial.[13] Rather than remaining on a safe plateau as in Figure 16, we may deteriorate experiencing a profound sense of personal decline.

The optimists say that you can find a satisfying plateau on the job if your off-the-job life provides a sense of challenge, encounters with the unknown, and mastery.[14] Such avocational activity must be more than drinking beer and watching television, of course. It should require discipline and commitment to a degree approximating what you brought to your career when thirty years old.

Some people are able to expand in their vocations virtually up to death. Artists provide rich examples of people who embraced new challenges into their eighties.[15] One of the best examples is Pablo Picasso who systematically rejected his past several times in order to develop anew. He began as a Spanish realist, learned French impressionism, left it to invent cubism, and gave that up for neoclassicism. Not every style was equally popular, of course, but each transition rekindled his creative fires.

Even for a genius like Picasso, each new encounter raises anxiety. "To venture," wrote Kierkegaard, "is to face anxiety, but not to venture is to lose oneself."

Changing personal skills.   The upper pyramid of modern corporations can be visualized as trisectional, as shown in Figure 17.[16] The primary job requirements in the lower section are technical—understanding equipment, procedures, processes, and techniques. Entry depends on the organization's judgment that you can perform or quickly learn the tasks. Rewards and promotions are based on a combination of seniority and performance in the primarily technical job. Some

Figure 17. Primary Managerial Skills

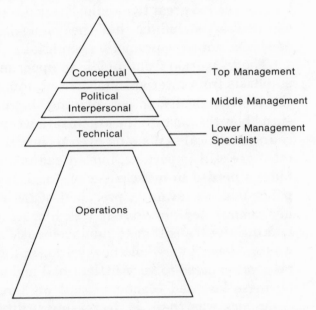

people will be satisfied with remaining at this technical level, but most probably aspire to advance upward to the middle sector of the upper pyramid at least.

The primary skills in the middle, however, are different: they are more oriented toward interpersonal relations and politics. To be effective at this level, you need to influence people, to work as a team member, and to build coalitions and cooperation. Of course, technical skills do not become suddenly irrelevant, but there is generally a shift in relative weight from the technical to the political as one moves up to the middle ranks.

This can be a difficult transition for many capable technicians. They find themselves promoted to first-line management precisely because they are the most technically competent. But upon entering management they may become anxious about the interpersonal requirements. The worst course of action for such a person is to ignore leadership requirements and attempt to do all the technical work alone. Unless he or she is an absolute superperson, the load will just be too great to handle. Failure is likely, with higher executives concluding that the young-specialist-now-manager does not have promotion potential.

The transition from middle to upper management shifts emphasis from interpersonal to conceptual skills: ability to think strategically, to perceive the "big picture," to understand how the parts of the organization can be integrated. Of course, political skills (and even technical skills to some extent) are still important, but an additional and rarer attribute is needed to make a successful transition to top-level, policy-making levels. A president of the Koppers Company has commented on what it was like as a young engineer making the transition to management: "As an engineer, I was suddenly in a whole new world. In those days, an engineer got exposed to very little. I had had a survey course in business law and economics, but all I remembered about economics was there is decreasing utility in adding more fertilizer to land. I didn't know how to read a profit and loss, or a balance sheet and here I was 33 years old. I had never done any significant philosophizing."[17]

These skill transitions suggest a lengthening of time perspective as one matures and climbs. The early, short-run anxieties of immediate task achievement become tempered by the longer-run interpersonal or political perspectives. Time must be carved out of the present to invest in relationships.

Successful conceptual people seem able to project their visions well into the future, to spend time now on activities they may receive little or no personal feedback on. Thus greater personal patience, longer-time perspectives, expanded ambiguity tolerance, and faith in the future become essential in managing at the top.

Conclusion

Managers have been dominated by the Newtonian view of time as constant, unvarying motion in which each interval is unique but equal. The activist ethic associated with this perspective encourages constant, short-range activity. It fosters guilt feelings when one is not busy and discourages speculation. The paradox for managers is that they need to relax a little in order to work more effectively—relax the intensity of their work on present problems and address themselves more to future possibilities. They need to value today less and tomorrow more.

Managers tend to avoid thought about the future because it is ambiguous. Clear-cut, programmed, short-run problems are difficult but satisfying to solve. In contrast, formulating wishes about the future, conceiving what we want the future to be, and perceiving the future as history is difficult and threatening.

The threat is twofold. First we tend to fear the kind of time necessary for such thought. It must be unstructured, open, and seemingly undirected—all attributes counter to time-haunted, efficiency-minded people. Wide-open time, like space, can be frightening. Second, incorporating concern about the future into the present necessitates clarifying what we really want, and this means defining fundamental values of management, organizations, and society. Such clarification is critical for all of our futures. An old American Indian proverb states, "All that is seen is temporary." The present is not unimportant nor is the world an illusion, but future-oriented, time-binding managers should have the kind of detachment often found in people who accomplish great things while refusing to be devoured by current events and present time.

My father spent thirty years as a manager in radio and television. His job was as time-pressured as can be conceived. Endless decisions on what should be broadcast over the network had to be made in minutes and seconds. When he retired, the large sweephand clock was removed from the wall of Master Control and presented to him as a gift. He came home and hung it on the wall of his living room. And then proceeded to die. He could not seem to find anything to do. The fishing he so loved before retirement had no allure.

Its tranquility had meaning only in contrast to his former job's pace. Sitting at home in retirement, he would compulsively check the clock or his watch to make certain of the time. But to him the time was meaningless.

Time need never be without meaning. As we grow older, our ultimate challenge is to invest it with importance by continually repeating an act of faith toward the future—by conceiving of possibility and devoting our most precious resource to its actualization. Thus, time is, in the end, much more than money; it is the stuff of life.

Drawing by Richter; © 1962 The New Yorker
Magazine, Inc. Reprinted by permission.

NOTES

Chapter 1 What Does Time Mean to You?

1. Marilyn A. Morgan, *Managing Career Development* (New York: Van Nostrand, 1980).
2. R. H. Knapp and J. T. Garbutt, "Time Imagery and the Achievement Motive," *Journal of Personality,* vol. 26 (1958), pp. 426–434.
3. D. C. McClelland, J. W. Clark, and E. L. Lowell, *The Achievement Motive* (New York: Appleton-Century-Crofts, 1953); and D. C. McClelland, "Business Drive and National Achievement," *Harvard Business Review,* July-August 1962, pp. 92–112.
4. H. B. Green and R. H. Knapp, "Time Judgment, Aesthetic Preference, and Need for Achievement," *Journal of Abnormal Social Psychology,* vol. 58 (1959), pp. 140–142.
5. R. H. Knapp and H. B. Green, "The Judgment of Music-filled Intervals and *n*-Achievement," *Journal of Social Psychology,* vol. 54 (1961), pp. 263–267.
6. David C. McClelland, *The Achieving Society* (Princeton, N.J.: Van Nostrand, 1961) (New York: Free Press, 1967), p. 327.
7. C. Benjamin, "Ideas of Time in the History of Philosophy," in *The Voices of Time,* edited by J. T. Fraser (New York: Braziller, 1966), p. 8.
8. As given in Reinhard Bendix, *Work and Authority in Industry* (New York: Wiley, 1956), p. 208.
9. Lewis Mumford, *Technics and Civilization* (New York: Harcourt Brace, 1934).

10. Marshall McLuhan, quoted in an interview in *Playboy,* March 1969, p. 53.

11. Michel Quoist, *Prayers* (New York: Sheed & Ward, 1963).

12. Michael LeBoeuf, *Working Smart: How to Accomplish More in Half the Time* (New York: McGraw-Hill, 1979).

Chapter 2   How the Present Tyrannizes

1. Combined from Ted W. Engstrom and R. Alec Mackenzie, *Managing Your Time* (Grand Rapids: Zondervan, 1967), p. 215; "Time at the Top," *Wall Street Journal,* August 13, 1968; and Leo B. Moore, "Managerial Time," *Industrial Management Review,* vol. 9, no. 3 (Spring 1968), pp. 77–85.

2. Sune Carlson, *Executive Behavior* (Stockholm: Strombergs, 1951).

3. Gerald Hickey, quoted in *Newsweek,* May 3, 1971.

4. Eugene E. Jennings, *The Mobile Manager* (New York: McGraw-Hill, 1971).

5. Laurence J. Peter and Raymond Hull, *The Peter Principle* (New York: Morrow, 1969).

6. Edward T. Hall, *The Silent Language* (Garden City, N.Y.: Doubleday, 1959), p. 20.

7. James MacGregor Burns, *Roosevelt: The Soldier of Freedom* (New York: Harcourt Brace Jovanovich, 1970).

8. David Sarnoff, quoted in *Nation's Business,* June 1966.

9. George A. Steiner, *Strategic Planning: What Every Manager Must Know* (New York: Free Press, 1979).

10. Clarence B. Randall, *The Folklore of Management* (Boston: Little, Brown, 1961).

11. J. Pfeffer and G. R. Salancik, *The External Control of Organizations* (New York: Harper & Row, 1978).

12. L. F. McCollum of Continental Oil Company, quoted by the editors of *Nation's Business* in *Lessons of Leadership* (Washington, D.C.: U.S. Chamber of Commerce, 1966), p. 128.

Chapter 3   Making Lists

1. Ted W. Engstrom and R. Alec Mackenzie, *Managing Your Time* (Grand Rapids: Zondervan, 1967).

2. Henry Kissinger, *White House Years* (Boston: Little, Brown, 1979).

3. Edwin C. Bliss, *Getting Things Done: The ABC's of Time Management* (New York: Scribner, 1976).

4. Joseph Trickett, "A More Effective Use of Time," *California Management Review,* vol. 4, no. 4 (Summer 1962).

5. Clinton Rossiter, *The American Presidency,* rev. ed. (New York: Harcourt Brace & World, 1960).

6. David Halberstam, *The Best and the Brightest* (New York: Random House, 1972).

7. Doris Kearns, *Lyndon Johnson and the American Dream* (New York: Harper & Row, 1976).

8. William R. Dill, Thomas L. Hilton, and Walter R. Reitman, *The New Managers: Patterns of Behavior and Development* (Englewood Cliffs, N.J.: Prentice-Hall, 1962).

Chapter 4   Keeping Logs and Diaries

1. Peter Drucker, *The Effective Executive* (New York: Harper & Row, 1967).

2. R. Alec Mackenzie, *The Time Trap* (New York: Amacom, 1972).

Chapter 5   Expanding Discretionary Time

1. Auren Uris, "How to Have Time for Everything," *Dun's Review,* August 1957, p. 53.

2. Peter Drucker, "How to Manage Your Time," *Harper's Magazine,* December 1966, pp. 56ff.

3. William Oncken, *Managing a Manager's Time* (New York: American Management Association, 1961).

4. Arthur M. Schlesinger, Jr., *The Imperial Presidency* (Boston: Houghton Mifflin, 1973).

5. George Reedy, *The Twilight of the Presidency* (New York: Norton, 1970).

6. Clark Clifford, quoted in *Time,* June 8, 1970.

7. Clarence B. Randall, *The Folklore of Management* (Boston: Little, Brown, 1966).

8. Robert Townsend, *Up the Organization* (New York: Knopf, 1970).

9. Richard M. Nixon, *Memoirs* (New York: Grosset & Dunlap, 1978).

10. Rosalind Forbes, *Corporate Stress* (Garden City, N.Y.: Doubleday, 1979).

11. Edwin C. Bliss, *Getting Things Done: The ABC's of Time Management* (New York: Scribner, 1976).

12. R. Alec Mackenzie, *The Time Trap* (New York: Amacom, 1972).

13. Peter Drucker, *The Effective Executive* (New York: Harper & Row, 1967).

Chapter 6 Fighting Procrastination

1. J. B. Rotter, "Generalized Expectancies for Internal versus External Control of Reinforcement," *Psychological Monograph* No. 609, vol. 80, no. 1 (1966).

2. George E. Vaillant, *Adaptation to Life* (Boston: Little, Brown, 1977).

3. Ernest Jones, *Essays in Applied Psychoanalysis* (London: Hogarth, 1951).

4. "How 179 Chief Executives Waste Their Time," *Business Management,* March 1968, pp. 12–14. The survey was conducted by Daniel D. Howard Associates, Inc., Chicago.

5. "Time at the Top," *Wall Street Journal,* August 13, 1968.

6. R. Alec Mackenzie, *The Time Trap* (New York: Amacom, 1972).

7. Leonard R. Sayles, *Leadership* (New York: McGraw-Hill, 1979).

8. Ross A. Webber, *Time and Management* (New York: Van Nostrand Reinhold, 1972).

9. Anthony Jay, *Management and Machiavelli* (New York: Holt, Rinehart & Winston, 1968), p. 136.

10. Webber, *Time and Management.*

Chapter 7 Tying Time to Objectives

1. George A. Steiner, *Strategic Planning: What Every Manager Must Know* (New York: Free Press, 1979).

2. Robert Heilbroner, *The Future as History* (New York: Harper & Row, 1960).

3. Ross A. Webber, *Management: Basic Elements of Managing Organizations,* rev. ed. (Homewood, Ill.: Irwin, 1979). The description of planning is derived from this text.

4. Peter F. Drucker, *The Practice of Management* (New York: Harper, 1954).

5. W. G. Bennis, *Organizational Development* (Reading, Mass.: Addison-Wesley, 1969).

6. James B. Quinn, "Strategic Goals: Process and Politics," *Sloan Management Review,* Fall 1977, pp. 21–37.

7. R. M. Steers and D. G. Spenser, "Achievement Needs and MBO Goal Setting," *Personnel Journal,* vol. 57, no. 1 (1978), pp. 26–28.

8. L. N. Redman, "Planning and Control and Accounting: Divide and Conquer," *Managerial Planning,* vol. 25, no. 1 (1976), pp. 15–17.

9. J. W. Humble, *How to Manage by Objectives* (New York: Amacom, 1978).

Chapter 8   How the Past Enslaves

1. A. D. Chandler, Jr., *The Visible Hand: The Managerial Revolution in American Business* (Cambridge, Mass.: Harvard University Press, 1977).

2. Allan Nevins with Frank E. Hill, *Ford,* 3 vols. (New York: Scribner, 1954–1963). See especially volume 3, *Decline and Rebirth.*

3. Alfred P. Sloan, Jr., *My Years with General Motors,* edited by John McDonald with Catharine Stevens (Garden City, N.Y.: Doubleday, 1964).

4. Joost A. M. Meerlo, "The Time Sense in Psychiatry," in *The Voices of Time,* edited by J. T. Fraser (New York: Braziller, 1966).

5. Elting E. Morison, *Men, Machines and Modern Times* (Cambridge, Mass.: M.I.T. Press, 1966).

6. Joseph Hall, quoted by the editors of *Nation's Business* in *Lessons of Leadership* (Washington, D.C.: U.S. Chamber of Commerce, 1966), p. 209.

7. Victor A. Thompson, *Modern Organization* (New York: Knopf, 1961).

8. Morison, *Men, Machines and Modern Times.*

9. Felix Kaufmann, "Hard and Soft Health Technology of the Future," *Technological Forecasting and Social Change,* vol. 5 (1973), pp. 67–74.

10. See *Report of the President's Commission on the Accident at Three Mile Island,* 1979, and "The Kemeny Blast," *Newsweek,* November 5, 1979.

11. Morison, *Men, Machines and Modern Times.*

12. Ibid., p. 137.

Chapter 9   Delegating More Clearly

1. J. P. Kotter, *Power in Management* (New York: Amacom, 1979).

2. Ross A. Webber, *Management: Basic Elements of Managing Organizations,* rev. ed. (Homewood, Ill.: Irwin, 1979).

3. Clinton Rossiter, *The American Presidency* (New York: Harcourt, Brace & World, 1956).

4. Arthur M. Schlesinger, Jr., *A Thousand Days* (Boston: Houghton Mifflin, 1965); and Peter Wyden, *Bay of Pigs* (New York: Simon & Schuster, 1979).

5. William Oncken, Jr., and Donald L. Wass, "Management Time: Who's Got the Monkey?" *Harvard Business Review,* vol. 52, no. 6 (November-December 1974), pp. 75–80.

6. E. Dale and L. F. Urwick, *Staff in Organization* (New York: McGraw-Hill, 1960).

7. R. C. Sampson, *The Staff Role in Management* (New York: Harper, 1955); and L. A. Allen, "The Line-Staff Relationship," *Management Record,* vo. 16, no. 9 (1955), pp. 346–349.

8. G. G. Frisch, "Line-Staff Is Obsolete," *Harvard Business Review,* September-October 1961, pp. 67–79.

9. Wendell French and Dale Henning, "The Authority-Influence Role of the Functional Specialist in Management," *Academy of Management Journal,* vol. 9, no. 3 (1966), pp. 187–203.

10. J. K. Baker and R. H. Schaffer, "Making Staff Consulting More Effective," *Harvard Business Review,* January-February 1969, pp. 62ff.

11. David A. Kolb and Richard E. Boyatzis, "On the Dynamics of the Helping Relationship," in *Organizational Psychology: A Book of Readings,* edited by D. A. Kolb, I. M. Rubin, and J. M.

McIntyre (Englewood Cliffs, N.J.: Prentice-Hall, 1971), pp. 339–353.

12. C. R. Bell and L. Nadler, *The Client-Consultant Handbook* (San Diego: Learning Resources, 1979).

Chapter 10   Handling Role Stress

1. Robert K. Merton, *Social Theory and Social Structure,* 1968 enl. ed. (New York: Free Press, 1968).

2. D. J. Levinson, "Role, Personality and Social Structure in the Organizational Setting," *Journal of Abnormal and Social Psychology,* vol. 58 (1959), pp. 170–180.

3. R. Ritti, *The Engineer in the Industrial Corporation* (New York: Columbia University Press, 1971); and W. Imberman, "As the Engineer Sees His Problems," *Conference Board Record,* vol. 3, no. 4 (April 1976), pp. 30–34.

4. Ivar Berg, *Education and Jobs: The Great Training Robbery* (New York: Praeger, 1970).

5. Laurence J. Peter and Raymond Hull, *The Peter Principle* (New York: Morrow, 1969).

6. R. G. Simmons, "The Role Conflict of the First Line Supervisor: An Experimental Study," *American Journal of Sociology,* vol. 73 (January 1968), pp. 482–495.

7. H. O. Pruden and R. M. Reese, "Inter-Organization Role Set Relations and the Performance and Satisfaction of Industrial Salesmen," *Administrative Science Quarterly,* vol. 17, no. 4 (1972), p. 601.

8. H. E. R. Uyterhoeven, "General Managers in the Middle," *Harvard Business Review,* March-April 1972, pp. 75–85.

9. R. L. Kahn et al., *Organizational Stress* (New York: Wiley, 1964), and J. M. Ivancevich and J. H. Donnelly, Jr., "A Study of Role Clarity and Need for Clarity," *Academy of Management Journal,* vol. 17, no. 1 (1974), pp. 28–36.

10. W. R. Dill, T. L. Hilton, and W. R. Reitman, *The New Managers* (Englewood Cliffs, N.J.: Prentice-Hall, 1962).

11. S. M. Sales and J. House, "Job Dissatisfaction as a Possible Risk Factor in Coronary Heart Disease," *Journal of Chronic Diseases,* vol. 23 (May 1971), pp. 861–873. See also Rosalind Forbes, *Life Stress* (Garden City, N.Y.: Doubleday, 1979).

12. A. O. Hirschman, *Exit, Voice and Loyalty* (Cambridge, Mass.: Harvard University Press, 1970); and E. Weisband and T. M.

Franck, *Resignation in Protest* (New York: Brossman/Viking, 1975).

13. R. K. Peters and H. Benson, "Time Out from Tension," *Harvard Business Review*, January-February 1978, pp. 119–124.

14. N. Gross, A. W. McEachern, and W. S. Mason, "Role Conflict and Its Resolutions," in *Readings in Social Psychology,* edited by E. E. Maccoby et al. (New York: Holt, 1958).

15. D. T. Hall, "A Model of Coping with Role Conflict: The Role Behavior of College Educated Women," *Administrative Science Quarterly,* vol. 17, no. 4 (1972), pp. 471–486.

16. J. Steiner, "What Price Success?" *Harvard Business Review,* March-April 1972, pp. 69–74; and B. B. Wolman, *Victims of Success: Emotional Problems of Executives* (New York: Quadrangle, 1973).

17. D. Moment and D. Fisher, *Autonomy in Organizational Life* (Cambridge, Mass.: Schenkman, 1975).

18. R. Alec Mackenzie, *The Time Trap* (New York: Amacom, 1972).

19. D. Wise, *The Politics of Lying* (New York: Random House, 1973).

20. Karl Albrecht, *Stress and the Manager: Making It Work for You* (Englewood Cliffs, N.J.: Prentice-Hall, 1979).

Chapter 11   Tactics for Survival

1. James T. McCay, *The Management of Time* (Englewood Cliffs, N.J.: Prentice-Hall, 1959).

2. B. F. Blake et al., "The Effect of Ambiguity upon Product Perceptions," *Journal of Applied Psychology,* vol. 58, no. 2 (1973), pp. 239–243.

3. H. Anderson, ed., *Creativity and Its Cultivation* (New York: Harper, 1959), and C. W. Taylor, *Climate for Creativity* (New York: Pergamon, 1973).

4. Alan Lakein, *How to Get Control of Your Life and Time* (New York: Peter H. Wyden, 1973).

5. J. H. Greer and A. Turtletaub, "Fear Reduction Following Observations of a Model," *Journal of Personality and Social Psychology,* vol. 6 (1967), pp. 327–331.

6. Ernest Becker, *The Denial of Death* (New York: Free Press, 1973).

Chapter 12   Time and Success

1. David C. McClelland, *The Achieving Society* (Princeton, N.J.: Van Nostrand, 1961) (New York: Free Press, 1967).

2. D. C. McClelland and D. H. Burnham, "Power Is the Great Motivator," *Harvard Business Review,* March-April 1976, pp. 13–110.

3. J. P. Siegel, "Machiavellianism, MBA's and Managers: Leadership Correlates and Socialization Effects," *Academy of Management Journal,* vol. 16, no. 3 (1973), pp. 404–411.

4. D. G. Winter, *The Power Motive* (New York: Free Press, 1973).

5. Michael Maccoby, *The Gamesman* (New York: Simon & Schuster, 1976).

7. Donald Frey, quoted by A. M. Louis in "Donald Frey Had a Hunger for the Whole Thing," *Fortune,* September 1976, p. 140.

8. D. J. Levinson, *The Seasons of a Man's Life* (New York: Knopf, 1978).

9. Eugene E. Jennings, *The Mobile Manager* (New York: McGraw-Hill, 1971).

10. E. Roseman, *Confronting Nonpromotability* (New York: American Management Association; 1977).

11. P. C. Chew, *The Inner World of the Middle-Aged Man* (New York: Macmillan, 1976).

12. Erik Erikson, "Identity and the Life Cycle," *Psychological Issues,* vol. 1, no. 1 (1959); and Erik Erikson, *Childhood and Society* (New York: Norton, 1964).

13. G. E. Vaillant, *Adaptation to Life* (Boston: Little, Brown, 1977).

14. T. P. Ference, "The Career Plateau: Facing Up to Life at the Middle," *The MBA,* July-August 1977, pp. 21–22.

15. Otto Rank, *Art and Artist: Creative Urge and Personality Development* (New York: Knopf, 1932).

16. R. L. Katz, "Skills of an Effective Administrator," *Harvard Business Review,* September-October 1974, pp. 90–102.

17. Fletcher Byrom, quoted in *Fortune,* July 1976, p. 184.

INDEX

164